MIL

Alison Prince hated school. "It was so boring," she says. "I spent most of the time dreaming up adventures—which never happened, of course. That's why it's been such fun to write stories about Mill Green, where they really do happen."

As well as writing, Alison Prince has worked in television and at the Zoo (serving teas at the Penguin Bar), has sold newspapers, gilded picture frames, run a smallholding (getting up at dawn to milk the cows), driven a cattle truck, painted scenery, made furniture and hitchhiked across most of Europe. She wrote and illustrated *The Good Pets Guide* for Armada and is also responsible for the delightful drawings in Armada's *Hello to Ponies* and *Hello to Riding* by Jane Allen and Mary Danby.

At present Alison Prince lives in a cottage in Lincolnshire "about the size of a teacosy", and has no idea what will happen next. That, she says, is what keeps life interesting.

ALISON PRINCE

Mill Green on Fire

An Armada Original

Mill Green on Fire was first published in the U.K.
in 1982 in Armada by Fontana Paperbacks,
14 St James's Place, London SW1A 1PS.

Printed in Great Britain by
Love & Malcomson Ltd., Brighton Road,
Redhill, Surrey.

Contents

CHAPTER 1

Trouble on the Bus

"The driver's going to be cross in a minute," said Danny Williams. "That's twice he's looked round."

Matt glanced over his shoulder. "It's Kevin Evans and all that lot," he said. "They've got their feet on the seat in front."

"And they're smoking," said Danny.

The bus swerved into a layby and stopped. The driver, a stout, middle-aged man with a red face, got out of his seat and made his way down the middle of the bus. "You boys at the back," he said. "I've told you before. Take your feet off the seats. There's other people got to sit there."

"Oh, yeah?" said Kevin Evans. Making no effort to remove his feet, he leaned back comfortably and folded his arms, his cigarette at a jaunty angle in his mouth. "Who says?"

"I do," said the driver angrily. "And you can put that cigarette out."

"You gonna make me?" asked Kevin from the free corner of his mouth.

"Yeah, go on, Grandad, make us put our fags out," said Micky Brent, grinning and flicking ash. He wore a leather jacket with fringes along the arms.

The bus driver's face was redder than ever. Kevin and Micky and the other Mill Green fifth year boys who sat in the back of the bus were nearly all taller than he was. "I'm going to report you to Mr Hazzard," he said. "What are your names?"

Kevin scratched his head elaborately. "Funny," he said, "But I can't seem to remember." His hair was very greasy and long strands of it hung down over his forehead.

Rachel Greenberg looked over the back of her seat at Matt and Danny and said, "They make me sick."

"Monday morning," Micky was saying. "Can't remember nothing, Monday mornings."

"They didn't ought to have mornings," put in Paul Arcot. "When I've left this dump, I'll stay in bed mornings."

"You'll have to get up and work, son, like the rest of us," said the driver.

"Nah," said Micky. "Work's for mugs. We'll be on the Social." All the others cheered.

The driver gave up. He walked back along the bus to his seat, his face crumpled with irritation. On impulse, Matt said, "Those three are Kevin Evans and Paul Arcot and Micky Brent. I don't know the others."

The driver stopped and said, "Thanks." He wrote the names down then stuffed his notebook back into the pocket of his dustcoat. As he started the engine there were shouts and jeers from the back of the bus and Kevin Evans came to see which of the small-fry had dared to do such a rash thing.

"Oh," he said, staring down at Danny and Matt, then at Rachel and Sue Eames who sat next to her. "Potter's lot. Right. We'll be *seeing* you." He cuffed Matt across the side of the head then lurched back to his place.

Matt and Danny got out quickly when the bus arrived at school. Red-haired Stephen Chuff who had been sitting across the gangway came to join them. "You'll have to watch it now," he said. "What d'you tell him their names for?"

"I'm glad he did," said Rachel stoutly.

"Me, too," said tubby little Sue Eames. "They think everyone's so scared of them, they can do whatever they like. Well, they can't."

"All the same," said Stephen, "you'll have to watch it."

"We'll be all right if we stick together," said Danny, who was smaller than everyone else and always looked untidy and dishevelled. "They can't beat up a whole gang of us."

They were walking across the paved area between the beds of low-growing shrubs which the caretaker hated because it was so difficult to get the crisps bags out from under them.

"This school's such a funny shape," said Matt. "At the school I went to in London there was just one big playground and everyone could see if there was any beating-up going on. But this one's all nooks and crannies." He stared round at the irregular, dark-timbered buildings without appreciation.

"Mr Hazzard said in Assembly it was supposed to look like barns or something," said Danny.

"The architect wanted it to fit in with the countryside," Rachel told him. "So he tried to make it look sort of village-y. Not like an institution. That's why it's got all sloping roofs."

"And that's why there's places where you can get done over without anyone noticing," said Matt darkly.

They came to the First Year door and went in. As it was the beginning of the summer term and very warm, nobody had brought a coat to hang on the rows of pegs. They went straight in to Mr Potter's room which, like most of the rooms in the school, had a sloping ceiling supported by double rows of girders with zig-zag struts between them. The girders were bright red but the rest of the room was painted white. The notice board had a timetable on it, and a list of fire regulations, a letter from Debbie Smart's French pen-friend and a CND poster. So far this term there was nothing else except a notice which said, "*Whoever pinched my pencil case, GIVE IT BACK. Michael Chalmers.*" Underneath it someone had written, "*You left it at home, you burk.*"

Mr Potter, one of the First Year form tutors, was sitting at his desk, studying a type-written sheet of paper. He had been running his free hand through his rather spiky brown hair, which now stuck up in erratic tufts.

"Hello, sir," said Rachel. "What's the matter? Your glasses are all steamed up."

"No, they're not," said Mr Potter. He took them off and peered at them closely. "Oh, I see what you mean. No, that's a blodge of Farex. I had to feed the baby this morning."

"Is she still teething?" enquired Rachel. "You didn't have another bad night, did you?"

"No, thank goodness," said Mr Potter, wiping his glasses and putting them on again. "Slept like a log. Look, go and sit down for a minute while I try to understand what all this is about." He indicated the sheet of paper.

"What *is* it about, sir?" asked Danny after a respectful

pause of about three seconds.

"Hang on," said Mr Potter, reading. He reached the end and said, "Oh, God. Self-sufficiency has broken loose."

"What has?" They crowded round him, trying to see what the paper said. Mr Potter got to his feet and flapped at them dismissively. "Everyone sit down," he said. And then, as nobody took any notice, "*Sit down.*"

He stared round the room fiercely until everyone was quiet then, holding the paper by its corner as though it was very hot, he said, "This document proposes some rather startling educational innovations."

"You what?" enquired Peter Box.

"Funny ideas on how to run a school," translated Mr Potter. "We'll talk about it after Assembly when we all know a bit more about it. Mr Hazzard's going to fill us in. Now, stay shut up while I do the register."

Matt took the register to the office before joining the rest of his class in the First Year common room for Assembly, and on the way back the door of the technical drawing room opened and Kevin Evans came out. "Ah!" he said. "It's little horror-bag!" He grabbed Matt by his tie and backed him up against the wall. He bent down so that his face was close to Matt's, the lank strands of hair hanging across his eyes. "You got yours coming, sunshine," he snarled, "and don't forget it!" He gave Matt a push which sent him flying.

The door from which he had emerged opened again and Mrs Abbott looked out. "Kevin Evans, I *told* you to get along to the Head's office!" she snapped. "Now—*get*!" With a furtive shake of the fist at Matt, Kevin did as he was told.

"Matthew Aiken, you should be in First Year Assembly," said Mrs Abbott.

"Yes, miss," said Matt.

"This morning," said Mr Hazzard, "I have something very exciting to tell you about." Matt, sitting on the floor with the rest of the First Year, gazed up at the Headmaster with interest. He was a tall man with a soft brown beard and a bald patch on top, and he seemed to have such a beautiful idea of how a school should run that Matt thought he must be constantly disappointed by what it was actually like.

"...very expensive," Mr Hazzard was saying. "Books, paper, everything we need, not to mention the little extra things such as trips to the theatre or to a sporting event."

"Bingo," Danny whispered.

"M'm?" said Matt.

"Bingo. Raise money for the school. Betcha."

"I believe in the old principle that God helps those who help themselves," Mr Hazzard went on. "It is no use sitting back and waiting for the Government to give us more money. It won't happen. But we are a community of people with many talents between us, and I am sure we can find a number of ways of helping ourselves. Now, some of these ways are well known. Sponsored walks, jumble sales, bingo—"

"Told you!" muttered Danny.

"But I think we can do better than that. Mill Green school is lucky in being built on a large site which was previously farm land. Some of it, of course, has become our school field, but quite a lot, as you all know, is still fairly rough. There is the orchard, over here beside the sports hall, and there is the big area between the front gate and the games pavilion. Originally it was scheduled for a swimming pool—"

Some cheering broke out and Mr Hazzard raised his voice.

"I say, 'was' because costs rose while the school was being built and the swimming pool idea had to be dropped," he went on. "But what I want to say is this. I feel that all our spare ground could very well be used to grow food. Our school canteen would benefit enormously and we could sell the surplus produce. We could also keep food animals such as chickens and rabbits, perhaps even a goat or some pigs. With this amount of land and hundreds of willing hands, we should be able to feed oursleves almost completely."

"Must be nuts," muttered Bill North, whose father was a farmer. "Can't make money on a little place like this."

There was a general babble of conversation despite hushing by Mr Potter and the other form tutors who sat on chairs round the sides of the room. Mr Hazzard held up his hand until there was silence. "I know that many of you already have a lot of experience at this sort of thing," he said. "Your parents may be farmers or smallholders and quite certainly they will know more about it than I do. But it seems to me that we can learn more in a real sense from an experiment of this kind than we can do sitting at desks throughout the summer term."

"Hooray!" said Danny cheerfully. Everybody laughed.

"I am perfectly serious," said Mr Hazzard gravely.

Rachel, sitting on Matt's other side, said, "I think it's a *lovely* idea."

"You would," said Matt.

"Exams, of course," Mr Hazzard continued, "will mean that the senior forms are tied up for most of the summer term. For that reason I am proposing that you younger people should be responsible for this project."

A movement outside the big windows caught Matt's eye. He turned his head and saw Ollie Withett, the assistant caretaker, lurch into view. He was pushing a wheelbarrow but when he noticed that Assembly was in progress he put it down and came close to the window, pressing his face against the glass so that his nose turned into a flat blob. Ollie was about eighteen and had thick black eyebrows which almost met in the middle. His shaggy hair stuck out over his ears, making him look, Matt thought, like an ape man.

"You will stay in your form groups for the first period this morning," Mr Hazzard went on, "and discuss this idea with your form tutors."

Ollie slowly blew a bubble of brilliant pink gum which spread hideously across the glass. Matt nudged Danny, who looked up and snorted with amusement. Mr Fox, the metalwork master, turned round to see what they were laughing at and found himself face to face with the black-haired apparition. He waved a dismissive hand but Ollie grinned amiably and stayed put. By this time the entire assembly was in fits of laughter and Mr Hazzard had given up trying to say anything. Mr Fox leaned close to the window and, under cover of his hymn book, gave Ollie a ferocious gesture which he obviously understood. He fingered the ropey gum back into his mouth, gave the smeared glass a cursory wipe with his sleeve and lumbered off with his wheelbarrow.

Mr Hazzard waited sternly for silence. "I would like a sheet of *sensible* suggestions from each form, handed in to my office some time today," he said. Then he sat down.

Mr Watts, the senior master, jumped to his feet. "Lead off!" he commanded. "And no talking!"

Mrs Gipsum at the piano plunged into "Country Gardens" and the First Year shuffled out.

Back in their form room, Mr Potter's class were making a lot of noise. There were several arguments going on about Mr Hazzard's idea but quite a few people were making a noise just for the fun of it.

"That caretaker bloke is nuts," said Matt.

"Fruit-cake," Danny agreed. "I don't know why Mr Hazzard doesn't sack him."

"Ollie's all right," put in Stephen. "He was here with my brother. Before Mr Hazzard was Head, that was. He came from that Children's Home over near Woolford and he was awful, George said. Used to smash things and steal things. But when Mr Hazzard came he said Ollie was deprived."

Mr Potter came in and said, "Quiet!" Nobody took any notice.

"Why was he deprived?" asked Matt.

"He was an orphan," said Stephen. "And he'd been to lots of foster homes but nobody liked him so he never had a proper family. But Mr Hazzard let him come in the office and gave him jobs to do and when he left he got him this job as assistant caretaker."

"Mad," said Danny.

"I think it's lovely," said Rachel. "He's ever so kind, Mr Hazzard."

"You think everything's lovely," said Matt with scorn.

"Settle down!" shouted Mr Potter.

"OK, boss!" Danny shouted back. John Beasley climbed over Felicity's desk on his way to his own and she hit him with an atlas.

"John, do stop behaving like an ape-man," bawled Mr Potter. "It's hell in here. *Quiet*, everyone!"

John gibbered and scratched and Felicity glared at him.

"Now," said Mr Potter when he could be heard. "About this down-to-earth scheme."

A babble of noise broke out at once and he held up both hands and shouted, "*Quiet!*"

"Look here," he went on when the din had subsided, "I can't be doing with all this row. Put your hands up if you want to say something and we'll keep it civilised. Imagine it's the House of Commons."

Several people laughed and Sue Eames said, "My Dad made me listen to that and it was awful. All shouting and yelling—much worse than us, sir!"

"Oh, dear," said Mr Potter. "Another illusion shattered. But anyway, too much noise makes my head ache."

"Poor old sir," said Rachel sympathetically.

"We must get *on*," said Mr Potter rather desperately. "What do you think about this idea? No—hands up . . . Bill."

"Most of your crops will come in the summer holidays," said Bill North. "There'll be nobody here to use them."

"There's a freezer in Home Economics," Sue pointed out. "We could pick things and freeze them—if we can get in the school, that is."

"Mr Hazzard thinks the place should be much more generally used," said Mr Potter. "He was saying at the last staff meeting that it seemed an awful waste to have the school closed all through the holidays. He'd like to see it used all the time by lots of different people—not just children. So I expect we could arrange to use the freezer."

Discussion broke out again.

"Anyway," Mr Potter went on loudly, "First point, what about summer holidays." He wrote it down. "What's next?"

"My brother might be able to get some piglets," said Stephen. "He works at a pig farm and they knock the runty ones on the head."

Several people made loud grunting noises and some of the girls said, "Ugh!" Mr Potter wrote down, 'Pigs'.

"It won't work," said Bill. "Not just pigs, I mean—the whole thing. Early peas should have been in ages ago and so should broad beans, and your ground isn't even broken."

"Can't your Dad lend us a plough?" asked Matt.

"I dare say he could plough it for you," said Bill cautiously. "And it ought to be mucked and harrowed, but I don't know if he'll do all that. I'll ask him."

"Number three—Bill North. Ploughing. With question mark," said Mr Potter, writing.

Felicity Banks suddenly piped up. "My Dad wanted an allotment but the council hadn't got one," she said. "So if he helped with the school garden, do you think he could have some vegetables sometimes?"

"Now, that's a new angle on it," said Mr Potter, scribbling. "A sort of co-operative with people sharing work and produce. I wonder."

"My Mum's got a lot of ducklings," said Stephen. She'd sell you some—fifty pence each."

Several people at the back of the room quacked loudly.

"But we haven't got any money," said Rachel, ignoring the quacking.

"I think that's what we ought to do first," Matt decided. "Raise some money so we've got a fund. Otherwise we can't even buy spades and things."

"Bingo," said Danny, nodding wisely.

"We could have a jumble sale," suggested Sue. "I don't mind going round and collecting jumble."

"I'll have a Bring and Buy sale," offered Rachel.

"Turnips would give you a crop in six weeks from sowing," Bill told them.

"How about a goat?" asked Peter Box.

There was an outbreak of bleating from the back of the room where the people who never said anything sat, and Mr Potter glared at them. "If you lot can't suggest anything useful, then at least shut up," he said.

"What about a cow?" asked a gloomy voice, and there was an instant chorus of mooing. Mr Potter leapt to his feet, his face suddenly bright red.

"I've had enough of this!" he shouted, striding towards the offenders. "You idiots are just a waste of everyone's time. A headmaster like Mr Hazzard is one in a million—most of them just sit there fussing about exam results and pouring out sherry for the governors. It's not his fault you've got to go to school, or *my* fault, for Heaven's sake! If it wasn't for the law of the country we'd chuck some of you out with the greatest of pleasure. John Beasley, wipe that stupid grin off your face! Can't you see," he went on, "that we're leaning over backwards to try and make life a bit more interesting for you? It would be a lot easier to dish out an exercise and have us teachers prowling about with big sticks making sure you did it. But you don't give a tuppeny damn, do you?"

"That's right," agreed Rachel, her curly hair bobbing as she nodded vigorously. "I think—"

"She thinks it's lovely," said Matt gloomily. Everyone laughed and Mr Potter made his way back to his desk. He sat down, still very pink, and ran his fingers through his hair.

"You shouldn't do that, sir," Rachel told him. "It makes you look like a hedgehog."

"Honestly, Rachel," said Mr Potter, "there are times when I feel as if you're my mother." He smoothed his hair down and picked up his sheet of paper. "Right. This is what we've got so far. Summer holidays. Piglets, Bill's Dad about ploughing, workers' co-operative perhaps sharing produce. Ducks, fund-raising, goat."

"Cow," said somebody, and this time there was no mooing.

"Cow," repeated Mr Potter, writing it down.

"Herbs," suggested Felicity. "For cooking. And we could dry them and use them in the winter."

"Or sell them," said Rachel.

"You want to spray it all down with Gramoxone first," said Bill. "Get rid of all your rubbish. Then plant main crop spuds and next year the ground will be much better."

"But we want to grow something *now*," said Matt. "Not next year."

"Outdoor tomatoes," suggested Stephen. "We might have some plants left over."

"You could grow marrows," said John Beasley suddenly. "Any twit can grow marrows."

"Marrows," said Mr Potter, writing it down. "And tomatoes, and Bill says main crop spuds."

The electric bell rang two long blasts to indicate lesson-change and everyone stood up, grovelling about for their bags.

"Thanks for your help!" shouted Mr Potter over the din. "See you this afternoon!"

"OK, sir." "'Bye, sir." They shuffled out. Matt checked in his bag to make sure he had everything he needed for Maths. Mr Watts took Set One. And there was no mucking about with him.

CHAPTER 2

The First Fire

"I'm going to the bog," said Danny at break time. "See you outside."

"O.K.," said Matt. He pushed through the double swing doors with the hordes of others and at once found himself surrounded unusually closely by people much bigger than himself. Looking up, he saw with dismay that they were Kevin Evans, Micky Brent and Paul Arcot. They hustled him round the corner and along the back of the building towards the Drama hall. Matt knew that there was a gap between the outside corner of the technical drawing room and the car maintenance bay behind the metalwork shop. Nobody ever went round there and it was not a nice place in which to find oneself alone with Kevin Evans and his friends. He ducked very suddenly and tried to run between them, but a large hand grabbed his collar.

"Silly," said Kevin, lifting Matt almost off his feet. He had caught a tuft of Matt's rather long fair hair in with his collar, and Matt's eyes began to water.

"Who's a slimy little git, then?" enquired Micky as they dragged Matt round the corner.

"I am," said Matt obediently, trying not to reveal how scared he felt.

Kevin slapped him casually across the side of the head and said, "That's for being a slimy little git." He pinned Matt against the wall and went on, "Got your dinner money today, have you?"

"Yes," said Matt.

"Hand it over, then," said Kevin.

"I didn't do you any harm," protested Matt. "The driver would have found out who you were anyway."

"Cheeky little sod," said Kevin. "What's he got in his pockets, Mick?"

Matt tried to struggle but Kevin twisted his arms behind his back and when Matt kicked him, kicked back so hard that he gasped with pain. Micky rifled his pockets expertly.

"Sixty-five pence," he reported. "Set of football cards. Half a packet of chewing gum. Snot rag—don't want that—penknife. You aren't allowed to bring knives to school, sunshine, don't you know that?"

Matt made no answer.

"Speak when you're spoken to!" said Kevin, jerking Matt's hands further up between his shoulder blades.

"Yes!" croaked Matt. He liked his penknife. It had two blades and a screwdriver, and he had bought it with his own money.

"Much too good for him," said Paul, taking the knife. He opened the bigger blade and held it near to Matt's face. "Lovely and sharp," he said.

"Got a shaky hand this morning, Paul?" asked Kevin.

"Terrible," said Paul.

Matt turned his head away but Paul followed his face with the knife.

"Say you're sorry," commanded Kevin.

"I'm sorry," muttered Matt.

"Louder!" He gave Matt's wrists another agonising push.

"I'm *sorry*!" shouted Matt desperately.

And at that moment Ollie Withett came round the corner pushing his wheelbarrow with a large shovel in it.

"Oh, hell," said Kevin. He released Matt's arms.

"It's only Ollie," said Paul, grinning. "He's all right, aren't you Ollie!"

"All right? He's bloody nuts," said Micky out of the corner of his mouth.

Ollie put his wheelbarrow down and took the shovel off it carefully.

"Whatcher doing, Ollie?" asked Paul, grinning. "Found some muck to clear up, have you?" He still had the knife in his hand.

"Yes," said Ollie slowly, frowning so that his thick eyebrows joined in a straight, furry line. "I think I have." He swung the shovel with astonishing speed, hitting Paul a fearful blow across the forearm and sending the knife spinning out of his grasp. A second sweep of the shovel caught Kevin in the ribs and knocked him sprawling.

"Blimey!" said Micky. "He's gone bananas!" He took to his heels and ran, closely followed by Paul and, when he had picked himself up, by Kevin.

Ollie put the shovel back in the wheelbarrow and retrieved Matt's knife from where it had landed in the grass. He wiped it on his jeans, closed it and handed it back to Matt, who said shakily, "Thanks."

"You all right?" asked Ollie.

"Yes," said Matt, rubbing his arms. "Thank you very much."

"Is it your knife?" asked Ollie.

"Yes," said Matt. "They went through my pockets." He still felt rather breathless.

"They take anything else?"

"Just my dinner money."

Ollie felt in his pocket and produced fifty pence. "Here you are," he said.

"Oh, no, it's all right," said Matt. "I'll be O.K."

"You can give it me back tomorrow," said Ollie. He took Matt's hand and put the coin into it then turned away and picked up his wheelbarrow. "I got some more in the house," he said, and moved off, unconcerned.

Matt walked back to the paved area slowly, surprised to find that his knees felt a bit wobbly.

"*There* you are!" said Danny. "Where've you been?"

"Oh, having a picnic," said Matt bitterly. And he told him all about it.

"I wish I'd been there," said Danny. The bell had gone and they were walking back towards the school.

"Fat lot of good you'd have been," said Matt, looking down at his small friend. "Still, I suppose they might have tripped over you."

Danny screwed up his face fiercely. "I could have—" He paused, seeking inspiration. "I could have bitten their ankles," he said.

At afternoon registration, Rachel was full of ideas about the Down-to-Earth scheme, as Mr Potter called it.

"You've all got to come to my Bring and Buy sale," she announced. "I worked it all out in Geography this morning. Everyone who comes has got to bring something and everyone has got to buy something. We'll have it at my house this Saturday."

"Won't your mum mind?" asked Felicity.

"Oh, no," said Rachel, surprised at the idea. "She never minds things like that. We could sell cups of tea."

"How much?" asked Danny.

"Five pence," said Rachel.

"I think I'll bring my own Coke," said Peter Box.

"If you bring it, you must put it up for sale," said Rachel firmly. "Mr Potter, are you coming?"

Mr Potter looked alarmed. "Me? Oh—I've got a lot on this weekend," he said.

"But you live in Tavenham, don't you?" said Rachel. "Not far from me. You can spare half an hour. Oh—I know what we'll do. Guess the weight of your baby. The winner could have Peter's bottle of Coke."

"No," said Peter and Mr Potter simultaneously.

"Rotten spoil-sports," said Rachel.

Mr Potter opened the register and said loudly, "Right! All sit down while I call this."

"It's the same as this morning," Matt told him.

"Is it? Good." Mr Potter called the list of names, marking a red stroke beside each one present. He wrote in the total, closed the register and gave it to Matt.

"I'll take it today," said Danny quickly.

"Really?" said Mr Potter. "You're very helpful all of a sudden."

"No," said Danny. "I've just got a thing about ankles."

He went out. Mr Potter gazed after him for a moment, puzzled, then turned to the rest of the class.

"We've been talking about the Down-to-Earth scheme during the lunch hour," he said. "Mr Hazzard likes the ideas you've suggested—or some of them, anyway. Do be quiet, John. We'll be sending a letter round to parents, but we'd like you all to talk about the scheme at home and ask your mothers and fathers for suggestions. Will you do that?"

Those who had heard nodded vaguely and one or two people said, "What?" Mr Potter stood up. "Tell your parents about the scheme!" he shouted. "And—" The bell cut him short and he sat down again, dispirited, as everyone went out.

"Never mind, sir," said Rachel as she passed him. "We'll make sure everyone knows."

"Thank you, Rachel," said Mr Potter wearily.

On the bus home, Kevin and his friends sat looking out of the window in a bored kind of way and the driver winked at Matt broadly as he got out with the others at Tavenham. Matt winked back. It was obvious that Mr Hazzard had given Kevin and the others a tremendous telling-off.

Danny was the only one who lived further than Matt from the bus stop so, as usual, he walked to Matt's house with him. As they approached it he said, "What's that notice board doing in your garden?"

"I expect it's the builder," said Matt. "Mum's having the roof done now it's spring. She said she didn't want buckets and ladders all over the place in the cold weather."

Sure enough, the board which stood in the overgrown front garden said in fancy letters, 'L. Gremmit. Builder and Decorator' followed by his address.

"Coming in?" asked Matt.

"Better not," said Danny. "Mum was a bit cross yesterday because I was at yours and I was late home for tea."

"O.K., then. See you."

"See you."

Matt went round to the back door, and saw what his mother had meant about buckets and ladders. There seemed to be a lot of both. Mr Gremmit was sitting at the kitchen table with Matt's mother, drinking tea. He wore a dark green boiler suit and a hat pushed to the back of his head.

"Hello," he greeted Matt. "Just let you out, have they?"

"That's right," said Matt.

His mother poured him a cup of tea and asked, "Have you had a good day?"

"Mixed," said Matt. "They've started a Down-to-Earth scheme."

"There weren't much down to earth about my school," said Mr Gremmit. "All up in the air with books and that, they were."

"Mr Hazzard thinks we ought to grow our own food," said Matt. "And keep animals and not ask the council for money."

"*Does* he?" said Mr Gremmit, interested. "Sign of the times, innit? Good thing, too. Young people these days expect everything handed to them on a plate."

Matt drank his tea while Mr Gremmit reminisced about the hard times he had had as a lad. "Well," the builder said at last, draining his cup, "better do a bit more, I suppose." He resettled his hat on his head to show that he meant business, and got to his feet. Then he added, "If your headmaster wants a bit of demolition timber to make a few pens and that, tell him to come and see me. Long as he can provide transport, I don't mind doing him a bit on the side. Know what I mean?"

"Oh, yes," said Matt. "I'll tell him. Thanks very much!"

Mr Gremmit nodded, pleased with himself, and went out.

"This school seems a lot more lively than Valley Road was," remarked Matt's mother as she cleared away the tea things. "Are you glad we moved here?"

"It's great," said Matt. Then, thinking of Kevin Evans, he added more truthfully, "On the whole."

"Mr Gremmit was telling me there was an awful fire this afternoon in a children's home near here," said his mother. "He heard it on the radio. Everyone got out safely—but what a dreadful thing to happen! Poor little souls!"

"Our assistant caretaker came from a children's home," said Matt. "Everyone thinks he's nuts, but I like him. He hit Kevin Evans with a shovel this morning. It was great!"

"Really?" Mrs Aiken sounded worried. "But why did he do that?"

Matt wished he had kept his mouth shut. "Well—I was getting done over," he said, "just a bit."

"By this Kevin Evans? Oh, *Matt*—but why?"

Matt explained reluctantly and his mother sighed and shook her head. "I thought when we moved away from London there wouldn't be so much of that," she said. "Why is everyone so *violent* these days?"

"It's just that they're thick and they hate school," Matt said.

"It's sheer bullying," said his mother indignantly. "And I think something should be done about it."

"You won't start writing notes or anything, will you?" said Matt anxiously. "It'll only make things worse."

Mrs Aiken gazed at her son doubtfully. "Well, if you're sure," she said. "But I still think it's absolutely dreadful."

In the bus the next morning, Kevin said loudly, "Funny about the fire, wasn't it?"

"At the home for nutty kids where Ollie Withett came from," chimed in Micky.

"Reckon he must have paid them a visit," agreed Paul.

"With a box of matches," said Kevin.

The other fifth formers laughed loudly.

Danny put a restraining hand on Matt's arm. "Don't say anything," he advised.

"I won't," agreed Matt. "It makes me sick, though, them saying things about Ollie. He's a really good sort."

"Ollie is a firebug," came a chanted chorus from the back. "Ollie is a firebug, Ollie is a—"

"Why don't you shut up?" demanded Rachel suddenly, turning round to look over the back of her seat. "And it's not a home for nutty kids, anyway, it's for orphans." Then she sat down again quickly amid cat-calls and boos from the rear seats.

"Good old Rachel," said Danny, grinning. He glanced back along the gangway and added, "They're not putting their feet on the seats today, anyway."

"Or smoking," said Matt. "I wonder what Mr Hazzard said to them."

"I don't think he could be nasty to anyone," said Rachel, kneeling up again so that she could join in the conversation.

"He's lovely. Our headmistress at the Junior was terrible. She made you feel naughty even if you weren't."

"I bet Mr Hazzard's tougher than he looks," said Danny.

Matt thought of the headmaster's gentle wispy appearance and said, "He'd better be."

"But if he isn't," said Danny thoughtfully, "There's always Mr Watts." And everybody groaned.

The first period that morning was Maths, and for one reason and another, Matt's attention wandered.

"Matthew Aiken, get on with your work," said Mr Watts crisply. Matt glanced rather blankly at his SMP book. He had forgotten to give Mr Potter the builder's message about demolition timber for the scheme. He stared at Mr Watts' bald head and neat fringe of dark hair thoughtfully. If it was anyone else, he might be able to get permission to go and see Mr Potter. Mr Watts looked up again from the pile of books he was marking and said, "What's the matter with you, boy? You don't usually look quite so gormless." Everyone giggled.

"It's about the scheme, sir," said Matt.

"The what?"

"The Down-to-Earth scheme. I was supposed to give Mr Potter a message at registration and I forgot."

"That is hardly my problem," snapped Mr Watts. "And I do hope that this outbreak of garden gnomery is not going to have a disastrous effect on the serious work of the school."

Rachel caught Matt's eye and made a face, and Matt returned to his perusal of Vectors.

In the next instant the fire bell went off with a prolonged shrill peal. Everyone sat up, putting their pens down with pleasure at the prospect of wasting some time, and Mr Watts looked annoyed. "All right, all right," he said irritably, "There's no need to make more of a fandango of this than you must. You know your route out—straight down the corridor past the canteen and through the middle door to the bus area. No running and don't talk. Stand, and line up by the door."

"We had a fire drill only last week," Danny said to Matt as they left their desks. "Funny to have another one so soon."

"Danny Williams, stop talking!" said Mr Watts. "And do your tie up properly, boy—you look a mess." He opened the door and added, "Lead on."

The bus area was full of people standing more or less neatly in lines while members of staff clustered round the school secretary, who was distributing the registers. Suddenly Sue Eames gave a squeal and pointed at the window of the chemistry lab, where a small trickle of smoke could be seen drifting out. "It *is* a fire!" she said. Heads turned to look and in a few moments the whole school was in a shuffling, giggly state of excitement.

Mr Hazzard climbed on a chair so that his thin figure was clearly visible to everyone, and held out his hands for silence. In a few moments they were all quiet.

"I am sorry you have been disturbed," he said. "There has been a very small fire in one of the labs but it has been dealt with. There is nothing at all to worry about. Class teachers will call the registers and then you can go back to your lessons."

Walking back to the classroom, Danny suddenly grabbed Matt's arm. "Look!" he said. On the wall above the closed shutters of the canteen was scrawled in crude blue felt-tip the message, "Ollie is a firebug."

CHAPTER 3

The Police Arrive

Matt went to look for Ollie at break time, and found him mowing the lawn outside Mr Hazzard's office. The ride-on mower went quite fast and Ollie was obviously enjoying himself. He came quickly down the straight side of the lawn, slowed for the corner, turned sharply and picked up speed as he approached the side nearest to the car park. Matt held up the fifty pence he owed him and Ollie came to a halt.

"Thanks ever so much," said Matt, handing him the coin.

"'sall right," said Ollie.

"I thought you were great with the shovel!" said Matt.

Ollie frowned. "I wasn't cross," he said quickly, as if he was being accused of something. "I only hit him with the flat of it."

Matt looked at Ollie thoughtfully, noticing for the first time the broad shoulders and big hands and the rather fierce blue eyes blackly outlined by their dark lashes, and said, "I bet it would be quite something if you *did* get cross."

"I used to," said Ollie. "I nearly killed a kid once. He was bigger than me, mind, but they had to take him to hospital. I did some awful things when I was a kid."

"I used to get into ever so many fights at my last school," said Matt.

"It wasn't at school," said Ollie, remembering darkly. "I grew up in a children's home. It happened there."

"The one where they had the fire yesterday?" asked Matt.

"Yes. And if anyone says I started it, they're lying."

"Why should they think you started it?" asked Matt.

"I was there," said Ollie. "I went to see Mrs Morecambe. It was my afternoon off."

"Who's Mrs Morecambe?" asked Matt.

"She was my house mother. She's all right."

Matt nodded. And then he remembered what was written about Ollie on the wall over the canteen, and wondered whether he had seen it. As if aware of Matt's thoughts, Ollie said, "That lot who were doing you over, they'd like to see me in the nick. I've had a bit of bother with them before."

"What sort of bother?" asked Matt.

"All sorts," said Ollie.

Matt tried another tack. "What was the fire this morning?" he asked.

"Somebody set a wastepaper basket alight and piled a lot of chairs over it," said Ollie.

"*Did* they?" Matt was fascinated. "Gosh! It couldn't have been an accident, then!"

"Accident?" Ollie laughed shortly. "What do *you* think?" Then he glanced over Matt's shoulder and the thick eyebrows met in a scowl. "Here comes trouble."

Mrs Abbott approached, cup of tea in hand. She wore a tweed coat, unbuttoned in recognition of the sunny morning, and stepped distastefully over the gravel in her high-heeled shoes. A whistle on a red lanyard bounced on her ample bosom.

"Matthew Aiken!" she shouted, "What are you doing here? All first years should be round in the paved area. As to *you* Ollie Withett," she added disparagingly, "*you* should be glad you've got a job to do!"

Ollie looked at her with loathing and went back to his machine.

"Matthew, get along at once!" ordered Mrs Abbott.

Matt turned to go, but glanced over his shoulder in case Ollie should look round or wave. But as Ollie drove away on the mower, his only gesture was to raise two fingers boldly into the air. And that, Matt felt sure, was more for Mrs Abbott's benefit than his.

At registration that afternoon, Mr Potter came in with a stack of duplicated notices.

"Shall I hand them out, sir?" enquired Rachel.

"Please," said Mr Potter, handing them over.

Matt inspected his and found that it was a notice of a

meeting for all parents and any other interested parties about the scheme. Reminded, he went up to Mr Potter's desk and said, "Sir, I know a builder who says he can give us some timber if we can collect it, for making sheds and things."

"Oh, marvellous," said Mr Potter. "Here—" He took the top sheet off a stack of smaller papers, "You can fill in one of these."

Matt read, '*Mill Green School Self-Sufficiency Project*'. Underneath was a row of dotted lines with headings beside them which read, Name, Address, Telephone number and Nature of Help Offered. Matt wrote down, 'Mr Gremmit'. Then he wrote 'Tavenham' and 'Free Wood', and gave it back to Mr Potter.

"I don't know his address or phone number," he said, "but I'll get it off the board in our front garden."

"Great," said Mr Potter. He stood up. "Quiet, all of you, and quickly!" he shouted. For once, everyone stopped talking. "I'm going to leave this stack of forms on my desk," he said. "Anyone who can help with the scheme, please take one and fill it in. Just name, address, telephone number and what you can do."

"Shall I do one about my Bring and Buy sale, sir?" asked Rachel.

"Yes, do," said Mr Potter. "Now—register."

As he was calling the list of names, John Beasley looked out of the window and said, "Coo, look! Here's the fuzz!"

Peter Box immediately joined him at the window. "Bet it's about the fire," he said.

"Sit down!" ordered Mr Potter. Peter sat down half-heartedly but John continued to crane his neck out of the window, which he had now opened. "John—sit *down*!" Mr Potter shouted. "That's better." He finished calling the register, closed it and gave it to Matt.

"Bet they've come for Ollie," said John.

"Why?" asked Matt, bristling.

"Started the fire, didn't he," said John.

"And the one at the home," agreed Michael Chalmers.

"He didn't," said Matt furiously. "I know he didn't."

"'Course he did," said Peter Box. "Police wouldn't have come else, would they?"

"Now, hang on," said Mr Potter firmly. "Nobody has proved anything against Ollie Withett and the least we can do is give him the benefit of the doubt. I don't want to hear any more of this idle gossip."

"Good old sir," said Rachel.

All through the afternoon, Matt wondered what was going on. He usually liked Art because Mr Pebblemarsh bounded about so enthusiastically and said funny things in his Liverpool accent, but today Matt could not get interested in his drawing of a smashed-in hub cap from a breaker's yard. He did not even mind too much when Mr Pebblemarsh said it looked like a half-eaten rice pudding.

R.E. was even worse because they had Miss Harker, who couldn't manage them at all. John Beasley kept flicking chewed paper pellets about and Peter Box made his Japanese watch play Greensleeves non-stop. Felicity got her crochet out and gossiped to Debbie loudly about last night's television. Rachel and Sue did a bit of work but even they got fed up because there was so much noise going on and played Hangman instead. Michael Chalmers offered to clean the board and, like an idiot, Miss Harker let him, and he wrote 'Manchester United' all over it. When Miss Harker tried to get the board rubber back, he threw it to Peter, and Debbie screamed because it hit her by mistake. And after that the rubber went from hand to hand in an endless game of Catch, with poor Miss Harker making grabs at it like a Pig in the Middle.

Matt and Danny had been having a long conversation about Ollie, though it was difficult to make themselves heard.

"They can't say Ollie did it if he didn't," Danny shouted consolingly to Matt, who was still angry about the accusations.

"No, of course they can't," Matt shouted back. "But—I don't know. People don't like Ollie. You should have seen the way Mrs Abbott looked at him."

"She's an old bag," agreed Danny. "But if he stuck two fingers up, you can understand her being cross."

"That was afterwards," said Matt. "And I don't think she'd know it was rude, anyway. She's ever so old-fashioned."

Several other people had joined in the paper pellets war and bits of chalk were flying about as well. Miss Harker was darting from boy to boy, trying to grab bits of chalk from their hands and saying, "Do please behave."

The door opened and Mr Watts walked in. An instant, out-of-breath silence fell, and Miss Harker tried to tuck in an untidy strand of hair which had come loose. She looked as if she was going to cry. Mr Watts stared round menacingly and said, "I will be back to speak to you in a few moments. Get on with your work. Chalmers, clean that filth off the board and sit down." Then he added, "Miss Harker, could I have a word with you, please?" and stood back to let her go out of the door in front of him. When they had both gone out, Danny whispered, "Bet he'll tell her off."

"Bet he'll tell *us* off," Matt whispered back, bending industriously over his book.

He was right. Miss Harker did not come back and Mr Watts went on at length about how disgusting it was to give an inexperienced teacher a hard time and how ashamed the school was to have such uncouth, bad-mannered, ill-brought-up and sadistic people among its numbers. Rachel and Sue began to look quite upset and even John Beasley didn't dare say anything.

"I shall stay here," Mr Watts went on, "until the end of this lesson, and I shall inspect each book to see exactly who has been working and who has not. And if any *one* of you dares to raise his or her head or say a *word* before the bell goes, it will give me the greatest pleasure to deal with the matter personally."

There was utter silence while he prowled along the rows, inspecting each book and jotting down comments in a small notebook which he kept in the top pocket of his jacket. Even when the bell went, nobody jumped up.

"Remember," said Mr Watts as he moved unhurriedly to the front of the room, "you are never alone in this school. Other people are always aware of what is going on. Next time Miss Harker teaches you, I shall expect a minimum standard of decent courtesy to be shown towards her. And, make no mistake, I shall *know*. Now you may file out quietly. Good afternoon."

With murmurs of "Good afternoon, Mr Watts," they shuffled out.

"He was wrong about one thing," said Matt as they waited outside for the Tavenham bus. "You *can* be alone in this school. I was yesterday, with Kevin and his lot. If it hadn't been for Ollie, I don't know what would have happened."

"Talking of Ollie," said Danny, "I wonder what *did* happen?"

He was overheard by Paul Arcot, who was lounging against the school wall with some other fifth formers. "Want to know what happened to the Wollie?" he said sneeringly. "Cops took him away, that's what happened. Shoved him in their car and took him off down the nick." The others laughed loudly.

Kevin and Micky came up to join the bus group at that moment, both grinning.

"Heard about Ollie?" asked Paul.

"Yeah—innit great?" they said, thumping each other on the back and almost choking with amusement. "What a laugh!"

"He must have started the one at the home, though," said Micky more seriously. "Must have."

"*And* the one here," Kevin reminded him. "'Course he did. Ollie is a firebug! Dead right!"

Matt clenched his fists tightly and looked murderous, his face flushing angrily under the mop of fair hair.

Danny said, "We'll just have to prove he didn't."

"*They* know who did it," said Matt, glaring at the fifth year boys. "They almost said so. I bet they started it themselves."

Stephen Chuff poked him in the ribs and said, "Don't try to be a bloody hero."

Matt was too angry to make any reply.

CHAPTER 4

Down to Earth

Matt was still eating his corn flakes when Mr Gremmit arrived the next morning.

"Cup of tea, Mr Gremmit?" asked Mrs Aiken.

"Wouldn't say no," the builder said cheerfully. He sat down at the table, pushed his hat to the back of his head and said to Matt, "They don't hang about at your school, do they?"

"Don't they?" enquired Matt, rather surprised.

"Young chap called Fox rang up soon as I got home last night. Wants to bring the school bus down to my place today dinner time. Says he'll take anything I've got."

"Mr Fox—he's the metalwork master. He's dead keen on anything like that. He's always scrounging round factories trying to get scrap metal for school."

"God helps them as helps themselves," said Mr Gremmit.

"That's what Mr Hazzard says," said Matt. "Oh, Mum, did you fill in that form? To say if you were coming to the meeting?"

"No, I didn't," said his mother. "I don't see that I can help much, really."

"But that's what the meeting's *for*, Mum," protested Matt. "If you don't come, you *can't* help."

"Looks as if I'll have to, then," said his mother. She signed the slip at the bottom of the notice, tore it off and gave it to Matt

"Seems like they mean business," observed Mr Gremmit.

Matt pushed the piece of paper into his sports bag with his books and said, "I'd better go. See you, Mum. Goodbye, Mr Gremmit."

Mr Gremmit, with a mouthful of tea, raised his cup in farewell, and Matt went out.

Danny was already at the bus stop, absent-mindedly picking at a hole in his jumper. When he saw Matt he said excitedly, "Did you see it had all about the fire in the paper?"

"Did it? Our paper doesn't come until after I've left," said Matt. "What did it say?"

"The headline said, 'Fire Scare at Mill Green School'," said Danny. "And then it said something like, 'Pupils left the building yesterday when a fire was discovered in a chemistry laboratory. Mr Hazzard, the headmaster, said there was no panic and the fire was quickly dealt with'."

"Did it say who started it?" asked Matt.

Danny shook his head and went on, "But it had a bit about Mr Hazzard saying the police had been called in because the school wouldn't tolerate vandalism."

The bus arrived, and Matt and Danny climbed in and sat in their usual seats, followed by Rachel and Sue and the others who got on at Tavenham. At the next stop, Stephen Chuff got on. He had a spade with him, a heavy, wooden-handled, rather cement-encrusted tool which caused a lot of amusement among the fifth year boys on the back benches.

"Gonna do O-Level ditch-digging, then?" shouted Kevin.

"Old Potter'll be all right," chimed in Paul Arcot. "He'll be taking prize marrows home to his wife."

"That's what it's all about, innit?" agreed Micky. "Slave labour. Potter's lot do the digging, Fox's lot do the hoeing, Miss Harker's lot spread the muck—"

"*On* Miss Harker!" suggested Kevin, grinning.

"And the teachers have free veg all through the summer," Micky ended. "Marvellous!"

"It's not like that!" Rachel said indignantly. "Only you're too thick to understand."

"Shut up, Rachel," muttered Stephen.

"You wanna watch it!" shouted Kevin. "Just because you're a girl, it doesn't mean you can be cheeky."

"Yes, it does," said Rachel, with a toss of her curly head.

When they arrived at school, the bus stopped behind another one in the drive leading to the bus park. Several more were waiting in front.

"What's going on?" asked Matt. "There must be something in the way."

Kevin, with the same idea in mind, shouted, "'Spect the fire brigade's here—Ollie's been at it again!" There were roars of laughter from his supporters.

As the bus edged gradually closer to the school, Matt saw that a large tractor and plough was taking up most of the space where the buses turned round. Ollie stood beside the tractor's cab, his shaggy hair looking even wilder than usual as he argued fiercely with the driver. Matt opened the window and leaned out so that he could hear what was going on.

"Nobody told *me* anything about ploughing," Ollie was saying. "And you can't leave this tractor here. The buses have got to turn round."

"Just show me the bit what wants doing," the tractor driver said patiently, "and I'll do it. Mr North said to be quick about it because there's a lot of other jobs waiting."

"I don't *know* which bit wants doing," said Ollie irritably.

"Where's the proper caretaker?" asked the driver, beginning to get annoyed. "You're only a kid—you don't know anything about it."

"He's having his breakfast," said Ollie. "He does the early bit then Mrs Amos cooks his breakfast and I take over."

Matt was not the only one leaning out of a window. From further along the Tavenham bus Kevin's voice came clearly in the sing-song chant, "Ollie is a firebug!" Several other voices joined in.

Ollie, already irritated by the tractor driver, completely lost his temper. Crimson-faced, he strode across to the bus and shouted up at Kevin, "Shut up, or I'll come in there and smash your face in!"

"Oh, yeah? You and who else?" said Kevin, who was safely out of Ollie's reach.

Ollie dived off round the side of the bus and wrenched open the door. Several of the girls screamed as his dishevelled figure bounded up into the bus and the driver got up and said, "Now, steady, son. He ain't worth bothering with."

"I'll kill him," said Ollie, struggling against the driver's restraining arm.

An incisive voice from outside said, "Ollie, come here a minute, please."

"It's Mr Hazzard!" whispered Rachel.

Ollie turned and looked at the headmaster then, with a last baleful glance at Kevin, got out of the bus. Matt saw that Mr Amos, who had now presumably finished his breakfast, had arrived on the scene, and several teachers had come out of the school building. Ollie and Mr Hazzard were walking across to the main entrance and Mr Potter was talking to the tractor driver, pointing to the rough bit of ground near the games pavilion. In a few minutes the tractor moved off and the buses were able to come in.

As Matt and Danny and Stephen were walking across the paved area towards their door, Mr Potter caught up with them. "That's a good spade, Stephen," he said admiringly. "Is it for the scheme?"

"Yes, my Dad said you could have it," said Stephen. "It's one of a lot he bought in an auction. He just wanted the muck fork and the post hole borer but it was worth buying the lot for what he paid."

"Is he a farmer?" asked Mr Potter.

"No, he's a postman," said Stephen. "But we've got four acres."

"Four acres!" said Mr Potter. "Whatever do you do with all that?"

"Mum keeps goats," said Stephen. "And we've got a lot of ducks and chickens and things, and we grow a couple of acres of barley every year. And the rest is just vegetables."

"Just vegetables," said Mr Potter faintly. "Heaven help us. And there's me with a garden the size of a Kleenex."

"My Dad hates gardening," said Danny. "So we have it all lawn."

"Does he like lawns, then?" asked Matt.

"No," said Danny. "He keeps saying he's going to cover it with concrete."

"My Dad didn't like gardens, either," said Matt. "It's one of the things he and Mum used to argue about."

"Doesn't he live with you now, then?" asked Mr Potter.

"No," said Matt. "There's just me and Mum."

"Is she coming to our meeting?" asked Mr Potter.

"I'm working on it," said Matt. "But she says she doesn't see what she can do. And she doesn't know anybody much."

"My Mum and Dad are coming," said Stephen. "Perhaps she'd like to come with them."

Matt nodded and said, "That's a really good idea. I'll tell her."

They reached the door and went in.

"Morning, sir!" said Rachel, who had arrived before them. "Look at my poster!"

Pinned on the board was a large notice which said, 'Bring somthing, Buy somthing! Sunnymead, Tavenham, Saterday, 25th April, 2 oclock'.

Mr Potter sighed. "I do wish you could spell, Rachel," he said.

"Oh," said Rachel, slightly dashed. "Have I got something wrong?" Then she brightened up. "Never mind," she said. "Everyone knows what it means. I've done three of them. Can I put one up in the entrance hall?"

"No, you can't," said Mr Potter firmly. "All sorts of people come in and out through there. If they see a misspelt notice like that on the wall they'll think we don't teach you anything."

"Well, you don't, do you?" said Rachel reasonably. "If I'd been properly taught, I'd be good at spelling."

"That's the Primary school's job," said Mr Potter hotly. "How on earth are we supposed to progress to the arts and sciences if you never learned to string two letters together?"

"I liked my Primary school," said Sue Eames dreamily. "We used to have lessons on the grass outside when it was hot, and I used to look after the hamsters."

"Yes, but did you *learn* anything?" persisted Mr Potter.

"How to look after hamsters?" suggested Matt.

Danny said, "Well, I went to the same school as Rachel and I'm a fairly good speller. I think it's just the sort of person you are."

"I can do other things," protested Rachel. "I mean, just look at your sweater, Danny—it's got a great hole in the elbow. If that was mine, I'd mend it."

"Well, I wouldn't," said Danny.

Bill North came in smiling rather smugly and Mr Potter said, "Bill, will you thank your father very much for doing that job for us? Mr Hazzard will be writing to him to thank him properly, but I just thought I'd say that we really do appreciate it very much."

"That's all right," said Bill. "I expect he'll harrow it for you as well, but you'll need to put some weed-killer down to get rid of the rubbish."

"You shouldn't use weed-killers," said Rachel. "They're poisonous."

"Of course they're poisonous," said Bill with contempt. "They wouldn't be much use if they weren't, would they?"

"My mother says if you upset the balance of nature you may start all sorts of trouble," Rachel insisted. "She won't even use a fly spray."

"You must have an awful lot of flies in your house," said Stephen.

"No, we don't—we kill them with a folded newspaper," said Rachel. "It's quite fun, really."

"Register," announced Mr Potter. "All quiet, now." Then as nobody took any notice, he added at top volume, "Shut UP!"

"Hush for sir," said Rachel. And, for a little while, the noise died down.

After lunch that day, Matt and Danny went to look at the bit of ground that had been ploughed up that morning.

"Fancy trying to do that by hand!" said Matt, looking at the long, fat rows of turned-over earth.

"Or even with a spade!" grinned Danny. Matt kicked him for being silly then resumed his inspection of the soil.

"You couldn't plant anything in it, though, could you?" he said. "I mean, it's so solid. Not a bit like a garden."

"That's what Bill means about harrowing it," Danny told him. "Ploughing just turns it over. Harrowing cuts it up and drags some of the weed out and makes it ready for sowing."

"Oh," said Matt. "I see." There was more to this farming business than met the eye, he decided.

The school minibus turned in through the gate and came

up the drive. Its roofrack was laden with a stack of rather rusty sheets of corrugated iron and the inside was crammed with timber. Mr Fox was driving it and Ollie sat beside him. Matt and Danny ran across the grass to have a closer look.

"Come to help?" asked Mr Fox as he stopped the minibus in the bus park.

Danny nodded and Matt said, "If you like."

"Great," said Mr Fox. He was a round-faced man with freckles and bushy red hair, and he had been the first teacher whose name Matt had remembered, because it suited him so well.

Mr Amos, the caretaker, came out and said, "The missus has just put dinner on the table, Ollie."

"I'll unload this first," said Ollie.

"No, you won't," said Mr Amos. "When she's got it ready, she likes us there to eat it."

"Off you go, Ollie," said Mr Fox. "I'll take the bus round to the back of the workshops. The timber can go in the woodwork store and we'll stack the sheets of tin outside against the wall."

"I'll do it when I come back," said Ollie, walking away relunctantly with Mr Amos.

"We'll help," Matt offered again.

Mr Fox smiled at him and said, "You're a bit small. We can use you all right, but go and see if you can rustle up some muscle-men, will you?"

"O.K.," said Danny. "Come on, Matt." And he set off at a run.

"Where we going?" asked Matt.

"Get Roger Smart—Debbie's older brother. He's in the sixth form. There he is!" Danny rushed up to a group of boys who were strolling along the paved area and said, "Mr Fox wants a hand!"

"He's got two of his own, hasn't he?" enquired Roger.

"He needs some help unloading the school bus," said Matt. "It's full of timber and things."

Roger looked at his friends and said, "Do we fancy unloading the bus?" They all sighed heavily and looked very bored. "Where *is* this bus?" asked Roger.

"At the back of the workshops," said Matt and Danny together. Roger smiled at their anxious faces and said, "O.K. See you there in a minute. We'll go through the sixth form common room. Quicker."

Matt and Danny beamed and rushed off across the grass. When they arrived, breathless, at the back of the workshops, the sixth form boys were there already.

"What horrible stuff," said Roger as he heaved a length of timber out of the bus. "It's got nails in it."

"We can't afford to pick and choose," said Mr Fox. "Now, you two first years, take the short lengths. I don't want you busting a gut."

With so many people helping, the bus was unloaded in no time and the sheets of corrugated iron were lowered carefully from the roofrack. "Two of you to each sheet, please!" called Mr Fox. "And mind your fingers!"

"Oh, yuck," said Colin Glazier, one of Roger's friends. "Thank the lord we're doing exams. I don't fancy playing these sort of games this term."

"Oh, I do!" said Danny cheerfully. "I think it's great!"

"That's the spirit," said Mr Fox. "Better sweep this bus out or the PE lot will have a fit if they take the marbles team for a jaunt." He went into the workshop in search of a broom.

"That was really an Ollie-type job," said Colin, looking at his dirty hands distastefully.

"He did load it all up," said Matt. "But he had to go and have his dinner."

"Thanks a lot, lads," said Mr Fox, sweeping busily.

"Any time," said Roger, turning away. "Funny chap, Ollie," he added.

"Going round the field?" asked Colin.

"Why not?" said Roger. They set off at the leisured pace which most of the sixth form adopted.

"Why is Ollie funny?" asked Matt, tagging along.

"I don't know—I just think he's a bit weird," said Roger. "He goes to our Youth Club and they all think he's weird there."

"Which one's that?" asked Danny.

"Chantry. It's in a big old house in Flaxton."

"I think it's rotten, not being able to join a youth club till you're fourteen," Danny grumbled. "What are *we* supposed to do?"

"Kiddies need early bedtimes," said Roger.

"Anyway," added Colin, "we don't want a lot of excited small fry running about the place. It's not a children's party."

"What do you *do*, then?" enquired Matt.

"Not a lot," said Roger. "Sometimes we just drink coffee and talk or watch television if there's anything decent on. But, like Colin says, you can't sit down and relax if the place is full of children."

"Sounds boring," said Danny. "I thought you played table tennis and had discos."

"Oh, we do," said Colin. "And there's a football table and a Space Invaders and bar billiards and all that. But I like it because it's somewhere to meet friends and have a chat. That's what's so odd about Ollie. He doesn't seem to have any friends."

"Doesn't he talk to anyone?" asked Matt, surprised.

"Oh, he talks all right," said Colin. "But you always get the feeling that he thinks you're a bit of a twit."

"Some sort of private joke," agreed Roger. "He just stands there and grins, and you wonder if you've got a smut on your nose."

"He's got an awful temper, too," put in Neil Blair from Roger's other side. "You know Kevin Evans in the fifth year? He was going on at Ollie one night, calling him Ape Man and all that, then he poured some Coke over him."

"Ollie poured Coke over Kevin?" asked Danny.

"No, Kevin did the pouring. But I never saw anything move so quick. Ollie caught his wrist and the glass went flying, and he spun him round somehow so he fell flat on the floor with his arm up behind his back, and Ollie kneeling on him. 'You say you're sorry,' he said, 'or I'll break your bloody arm'. And I think he would have, too."

"*Did* Kevin say he was sorry?" asked Matt.

"You bet," said Roger. "He didn't have much option."

"No wonder Kevin doesn't like him," said Matt.

"Kevin's been trying to get his own back for months," said Neil.

They came round the side of the building and out on to the field, and saw that the bell must have gone, for people were walking back towards the school in twos and threes and bigger groups. "It looks like iron filings drawn by a magnet," said Roger as he gazed rather condescendingly at the scene. Matt said, "Is that what Mr Watts means by 'filing in quietly'?"—and ducked to avoid the cuff which Roger aimed at his head.

"Crawl back in your apple," said Colin.

Matt and Danny ran off to their door and Roger said indulgently, "Some of these little kids in Potter's lot aren't too bad, are they?"

"Don't encourage them," said Colin with a shudder.

When Matt and Danny went out to the bus that night, Ollie was waiting for them, arms folded and scowling fiercely.

"Hello," said Matt.

"What d'you want to unload the bus for?" asked Ollie. "That's my job."

"Mr Fox asked us," explained Matt. "I think he wanted to have the bus empty in case someone had to use it this afternoon."

"That's a load of cobblers," said Ollie. "It's been stood in the car park all afternoon. Makes me look a twit, doesn't it, kids doing my job."

"I'm sorry," said Matt, confused. "I didn't think—"

"No," said Ollie bitterly. "People don't." And he walked away angrily, ignoring Matt's apologies.

"Funny bloke," said Danny, wrinkling his nose.

Matt was feeling rather hurt. "I can see what he means, now I come to think of it," he said. "But Mr Fox wanted it unloaded. If we hadn't helped, someone else would."

"The sixth formers did most of it, anyway," said Danny. He thought for a moment, then added, "I wonder what the police said to Ollie?"

Matt's face turned red. "Don't *you* start!" he said.

"No," said Danny mildly. "I'm not starting. I just wondered, that's all."

CHAPTER 5

Ollie Loses His Temper

"Tea, Mr Gremmit!" called Matt's mother.

"Right!" The builder came down his ladder at once, gave his boots a cursory wipe on the doormat and settled himself in his usual place at the table.

"Mr Fox was ever so pleased with the stuff you gave him," said Matt, passing Mr Gremmit the sugar.

"Ta," said the builder, stirring. "No skin off my nose, really. You replace old stuff with new and the people always want the place left clean and tidy so you take their old stuff with you. All very well, but it clutters up the yard something chronic. I told that boy he can give me a hand in the evenings if he wants—sort the place out a bit."

"Ollie?" asked Matt.

"Yes, that's him," said Mr Gremmit. "Looks like a gorilla, doesn't he?"

"I like him," said Matt.

"Oh, he's all right," the builder agreed readily. "I'm not saying anything against the lad. Just a bit hairy, that's all."

"You'll be glad of some help," said Matt's mother. "Things do get untidy, don't they? It's bad enough with just a small house."

"They certainly do," said Mr Gremmit. "He's got a motor bike, see, so there's no need to run about fetching him. And he doesn't want a silly amount of money. Most kids these days want more than I make myself."

"Unreasonable," said Mrs Aiken. The telephone rang and she went to answer it, and while she was away Matt told Mr Gremmit about the fire scare and how Kevin and his friends were trying to blame Ollie for it. "But he didn't do it," he added. "I know he didn't. He just isn't that kind of person."

"Never can tell," said Mr Gremmit. "I knew a chap once,

looked as respectable as you like, nice suit, tie, the lot. Well-spoken chap he was, too. Used to be Transport Manager for Greens—big electrical firm. Well! The stuff he knocked off. Shiploads of it, the police found. But they didn't suspect him for years."

"That's different," said Matt. "Ollie *doesn't* look respectable. But he's all right."

Mr Gremmit nodded at him approvingly. "That's right, mate," he said. "You stick up for your friend. I like to hear it."

Matt's mother came in, smiling. "Isn't that nice!" she said. "That was a Mrs Chuff on the phone, asking if I'd like to go with them to the parents' meeting at the school tomorrow. Her son is in your class, isn't he, Matt?"

"Oh, Stephen. Yes, he said he'd ask them to pick you up if they were going," said Matt.

His mother turned slightly pink as she said, "How funny to have one's children organising one's life! Makes you realise they're growing up."

"They do," said Mr Gremmit. He passed his cup across for a refill.

The next morning, Mr Potter stared round his classroom and said, "We'll have to do something about this."

Felicity's desk was stacked with egg-trays and a large, rather cobwebby galvanised iron chicken drinker stood in the middle of the floor. Stephen's spade still stood against the wall and he had brought several packets of seed with rolled-over tops because some of the contents had been used. And Bill North was holding a broad-bladed potato fork which he said was antique.

"Not that I *mind* the place looking like an auction yard," Mr Potter went on, "but other people use this room from time to time and some of them are not quite such keen Down-to-Earthers as we are."

Danny grinned and said, "Mr Watts, for instance."

"Name no names," said Mr Potter darkly. "A nod's as good as a wink to a blind horse."

Rachel beamed broadly at this and said, nudging Sue, "Isn't Mr Potter lovely!"

"Pack it in, Rachel," said Stephen. "You shouldn't say things like that."

"Why not?" protested Rachel. "I wasn't being rude!"

"Yes, you were," said Bill North. "It's not respectful, talking to a teacher like that."

"He doesn't mind," said Rachel. "Do you, sir?"

Mr Potter blushed slightly and said, "Actually, Rachel, it can be a bit embarrassing sometimes. I mean, I'd like all of us to be on good terms but there are some members of staff who think—well—that teachers ought to have a bit more dignity. Or something."

Rachel sat back in her desk and folded her arms, offended. "That's blooming school all over," she said. "They just want you to keep quiet and do as you're told. Nobody cares what you're *like*. Not a bit."

"Why should they?" said Bill. "That's not their job."

"Well, I think people are people," declared Rachel, "and it doesn't make any difference if one person happens to be a teacher and another happens to be a schoolchild."

"I agree with you," said Mr Potter, "but not everyone shares your civilised attitude, Rachel. What about the rowdies at the back?"

The conversation had been going on against a background of steady noise from the people at the back of the room, who were not aware that they were being talked about.

"Oh, *them*," said Rachel.

"They'll always muck about whatever you do," said Stephen Chuff, "so why bother?"

"But they spoil it for everyone else," put in Sue. "Like in Miss Harker's lesson the other day—we all got in a row."

"Oh, yes, I heard about that," said Mr Potter. "Mr Watts was very annoyed. I was going to have a word to say about it before the next R.E. lesson."

"I still don't think schools ought to be so stuffy," said Rachel obstinately. "Mr Watts is good at keeping people shut up and Miss Harker is bad at it, but I still like Miss Harker better."

"I don't," said Danny. "If she calls herself a teacher, she

ought to be able to manage us." He tucked in an unravelling edge of his sleeve, looking smug.

"That's what she's paid for," agreed Bill.

"Oh, dear," sighed Mr Potter. "What a tough lot you are." He glanced at his watch and added, "We must get on—I haven't called the register yet. I wonder if we can store our Down-to-Earth stuff in Ollie's shed?"

"Shall I ask him?" said Matt.

"No, I think I'd better," said Mr Potter. "Thanks for the offer, but I suppose it ought to be a sort of official enquiry."

Rachel groaned and said, "There you go again," but Mr Potter pretended not to hear. He opened the register, took his blue and red pens out of his pocket and began to call the names.

During Metalwork, Matt saw Mr Potter approach Ollie, who was sweeping up the path outside the Metalwork room. He did not hear Mr Potter's question, but Ollie shook his head angrily and said, "I can't have a lot of stuff in my shed. That's *my* place."

"Just for a bit, until we find somewhere else," said Mr Potter.

Ollie's face turned red. "Just because there's some daft idea about getting the kids to grow things, you all start pushing me about," he shouted. "Put things in my shed, use my tools, bring tractors in without saying a word. Bloody marvellous. Next thing, it'll be, oh, we don't need Ollie any more, the kids can do his job, save the school a bit more money. You really know how to make people feel wanted, don't you?"

He was talking so loudly that everyone in the room could hear him. Mr Potter noticed the row of interested faces looking out from the metalwork room and put his hand on Ollie's arm to try and draw him out of earshot. Ollie flung up his arm to shake off Mr Potter's hand and shouted, "Just leave me alone, will you?"

"Look, there's no need to be unreasonable," said Mr Potter.

"Bloody well *is* need," raged Ollie. "*I* know when I'm not wanted! Sweep your own path, Mr Schoolmaster, since you're so good at Do-it-Yourself!" He thrust the broom into

Mr Potter's hand and stormed off across the grass to cheers from the metalwork room, quickly suppressed by Mr Fox.

Danny grinned at Matt and said, "You've got some funny friends!

Matt said stoutly, "Well, I can see how Ollie feels. It must look as if we're trying to do him out of a job." But he glanced uneasily out of the window at Mr Potter marching towards Mr Hazzard's office with Ollie's broom in his hand. It was not easy, he thought, for anyone to think of Ollie as a friend.

At afternoon registration Mr Potter said, "We have decided to store anything brought for the Down-to-Earth scheme in the games pavilion."

"Doesn't Mr Ellis mind?" asked Rachel. "What about all his footballs and things?"

"They're kept in the cupboards by the gym," Danny told her. "There's nothing much in the pavilion except cricket nets and that sort of thing."

"Oh. Well, that's all right, then," said Rachel cheerfully.

Matt thought of Ollie's furious face and smiled. Obviously Mr Ellis was easier to persuade than Ollie.

"So anyone who's brought a contribution can take it across there now," Mr Potter went on. "Mr Ellis is over there to see that the stuff's just where he wants it."

Almost everyone stood up.

"It doesn't take *all* of you to carry things!" shouted Mr Potter. "Just the people who brought something." When some order was restored and the pavilion group had gone out he went on, "I do wish you weren't so silly, you lot. Every time there's a chance to do something daft, you take it."

"Didn't you, when you were at school, sir?" asked Sue

"School's boring," said John Beasley.

"Oh, all right," said Mr Potter. "Don't keep on. I just think that, since we've all got to put up with it as best we can, it would be a help if you'd stop seizing every opportunity to go galloping off like mad things, that's all."

Several people shrugged, conceding the point, and Rachel sprang to Mr Potter's defence. "You can't be more reasonable than that," she declared.

Matt, looking out of the window, saw that Stephen Chuff,

on his way to the pavilion with the others, had been waylaid by Kevin Evans. The conversation between them did not last long, but Kevin went off laughing maliciously and Stephen looked annoyed. The bell went for the start of afternoon school before the pavilion party were back, so Matt did not get a chance to ask Stephen what Kevin had said.

In her room on the first floor, Mrs Abbott stared round at the depleted numbers seated before her and said, "Where are the rest of you?"

"Taking some things to the pavilion," explained Matt. "Mr Potter told them to."

"I fail to see why these activities should interfere with my history lesson," said Mrs Abbott. The door opened and Stephen and the others came in. "We've been—" began Stephen.

"I know where you've been," interrupted Mrs Abbott. "I do not require any excuses." As the late-comers went to sit down she added fiercely, "I do, however, expect an apology!"

"Sorry we're late, miss," they muttered dutifully.

"I should think so. Now you may sit down. And in future, no matter *what* you are called upon to do, you will be in time for my lessons, do you understand?"

"Yes, miss."

"Right. Now you may remember that last week we started some work on the people who invented anaesthetics."

With great daring, Matt caught Stephen's eye and looked enquiring, pointing a finger towards the field to indicate that he wanted to know what Kevin had said. Stephen, failing to understand, looked completely blank. Cautiously, Matt tore a page out of the back of his general notebook and wrote on it, "What did Kevin say?" He folded it and nudged Danny, who sat beside him. "Stephen," he whispered.

Danny passed it over and Stephen unfolded the note. He wrote a reply below Matt's question then refolded the note and gave it back to Danny.

"*Thank* you!" said Mrs Abbott, pouncing. Matt gave Stephen a murderous look. Idiot! He could have been a bit more careful. Mrs Abbott opened the note and read it. Her eyebrows rose. "Most interesting," she said. Then she glanced over the top of her glasses at Stephen. "And to whom," she enquired, "was this missive directed?"

"Nobody," said Stephen, blushing to the roots of his red hair.

"Don't be stupid, boy!" snapped Mrs Abbott. "People don't write notes to nobody. Danny Williams, was it meant for you?"

"No, miss!" said Danny innocently.

"Matthew Aiken?"

"Er, yes," admitted Matt.

"Right," said Mrs Abbott crisply. "You can come and see me at the end of the lesson. Meanwhile, you can bring your chair and sit over here by the window where I can keep an eye on you, since you are so untrustworthy."

Carrying his chair past Mrs Abbott's desk, Matt tried to see what the note said, but she had refolded it. He prickled with curiosity for the rest of the lesson and when the bell went he was still too full of speculation to worry much about what Mrs Abbott said to him. Oddly, she did not seem very cross. She handed him the note and said, "What does this mean?"

Matt unfolded the note and read it. Under his original question Stephen had written, "Ollie will burn down Gremmit's yard. Just you wait." He looked up. Mrs Abbott was staring at him with her lips pursed. He shrugged. "It means what it says," he said. "Only it's not true. Kevin hates Ollie and so he—"

"I don't want to hear about any silly quarrels," interrupted Mrs Abbott. "Who is Gremmit?"

"He's a builder," said Matt. "He's working at our house and he gave Mr Fox lots of stuff for the Project."

"And where does Ollie Withett come in?"

"Mr Gremmit asked him to help tidy up his yard in the evenings," said Matt reluctantly. "But—"

"I see." Mrs Abbott smiled. "All right, Matthew, you can go."

"But Ollie wouldn't—" began Matt again.

"You can *go*," repeated Mrs Abbott.

Matt went out of the room, frowning. He felt that he had done Ollie a terrible disservice.

CHAPTER 6

Another Fire!

Mr Potter was on duty outside the next day. He saw Matt sitting on a bench with Danny, and beckoned. "Can I have a word for a minute, Matt?" he said.

Matt went over. "Want me to take your tea mug back, sir?" he enquired.

"No. Well, yes, but later. What I want to know is, what's all this about Ollie and the builder's yard? Mrs Abbott seems to think there's something quite serious going on."

"She's got it all wrong," said Matt. And he explained carefully how Kevin Evans didn't like Ollie and wanted to get even with him for a lot of old scores. Mr Potter listened, frowning. At last he said, "You can't prove all this, Matt, can you?"

"No," Matt admitted. "But it's so unfair, sir. Everyone thinks Ollie is nuts. Even I thought so at first. But I know he isn't now. I'm sure he isn't."

"M'm," said Mr Potter doubtfully. "I hope you're right. Nuts or not, Ollie's got a pretty short temper."

Matt remembered Ollie's furious face as he had argued in defence of his shed, and sighed. It was not easy to stick up for Ollie.

"Don't forget," Mr Potter went on, "that some of our fifth year lads are in the same boat in a way. And not just Kevin Evans and his lot, either. There are several others. People are ready to accuse *them* of things, too. It's a question of giving a dog a bad name, isn't it?"

"Yes," said Matt relunctantly, "But—"

"I know it's difficult," interrupted Mr Potter, "But I do think it's important to try and see things straight. It's so easy to get carried away, you see. Friendship demands a kind of loyalty—O.K., that's fine." He stared into his empty tea mug. "But loyalty is a difficult thing to put limits on. You are loyal to your friend. A soldier is loyal to his country. Everyone accepts that. But it didn't stop us turning round after the last war and saying to the Germans, 'You should not have done what you did. You should not have been so loyal to your leaders that you obeyed them without question.' Do you see what I mean?"

"Yes, of course," said Matt, a little irritated. "But the Germans were doing awful things to the Jews. My Mum told me all about it. But that's different. It's not like sticking up for someone when everyone else is running him down."

"Of course not," agreed Mr Potter. "But you can see what I'm getting at. I know it's difficult, but I'm just trying to say that you mustn't let your judgement be clouded by liking someone, that's all."

Matt felt his face turning red with anger. He pictured Ollie's big hands and the straight blue eyes under the shaggy brows, and wanted to tell Mr Potter exactly what he thought of his good advice. Adults had this awful way of expressing their opinions as though they were absolutely correct, while *your* opinions, they implied, were just plain wrong. Silly, childish mistakes. And teachers were the worst of the lot.

"I'll take your cup back," he said. And, not looking at Mr Potter, he grabbed the mug and fled.

That afternoon, Matt got off the bus with Stephen Chuff. After another telephone call, his mother had arranged with Mrs Chuff that Matt should stay with Stephen and his older brother George while she and the Chuffs went to the parents' meeting at school. Matt thought this was an excellent idea. Being an only child, he often felt rather bored with his own company.

"What were you talking to old Potter about?" enquired Stephen as they walked home to his house.

"I wasn't," said Matt. "He was talking to me. He's one of the anti-Ollie brigade."

"You can't blame him," said Stephen. "Ollie was ever so rude. And he did tell him to sweep his own path!" He grinned as he thought of it.

"Ollie wouldn't set things on fire, though," objected Matt. "I know he wouldn't."

"I don't see why you're so sure," said Stephen.

Matt frowned, trying to find words to express the way he felt about Ollie. It was very difficult. "I just—like him," he said lamely. "I like the way he looks and the way he *is*. He's all right."

Stephen looked at his friend with amusement. "You're as daft as he is," he said. Matt shrugged and tried not to smile. He wouldn't mind being daft like Ollie.

Stephen's house was a pink-washed cottage standing quite near the road. A cart track beside the house led to a group of outbuildings behind it and beyond that there was a big vegetable garden and a fenced paddock, then open fields.

"Gosh!" said Matt. "Do you own all this?"

"Only as far as the barley," said Stephen, pointing to the short green stuff on the far side of the paddock.

"It looks like grass to me," said Matt. "I thought barley was a sort of corn with whiskers on.'

"It is," said Stephen. "But it's got to *grow*, stupid! It won't be ready to harvest until August."

"Oh," said Matt.

They walked past the neat rows of vegetable plants and leaned on the fence, staring at the three goats in the paddock. "They're all different sorts," said Matt.

"That's right," agreed Stephen. "That's Mabel, the white one—she's a Saanen. The brown and white one's a Toggenburg called Betsy and the one with the floppy ears is an Anglo Nubian, Cleopatra."

"Do you milk them all?" asked Matt.

"Mum does. I help sometimes. And I usually feed the kids."

"Kids? Where are they?"

"In the goat shed. We take them away from their mothers and bottle feed them, otherwise they'd take all the milk and we'd have none to sell."

"Oh," said Matt. "It's very complicated, isn't it!"

They walked back to the buildings and found Stephen's mother feeding a large sow and her litter of piglets.

Matt eyed the sow with respect. "Isn't she huge!" he remarked. "I never knew pigs were so big."

"Oh, yes, they're whoppers when they're full grown," agreed Mrs Chuff. "Most of them are killed for pork when they're much smaller than her, you see. When they weigh about a hundred and twenty pounds."

Matt nodded and tried to look as if he knew how big a pig weighing a hundred and twenty pounds would be. He wondered whether Mr Hazzard would know. Then he said, "There a lot to learn about this sort of thing, isn't there?"

Mrs Chuff laughed. "Quite a bit," she said. "Would you like to help Stephen feed the kids? I've put the bottles ready, Stephen—standing in hot water in the kitchen."

The kids sucked furiously at the bottles, ears laid back and eyes blissfully closed. "Put your hand over the neck of the bottle," Stephen advised, "so you're holding the teat on. Sometimes they suck it right off and you get milk all over the place."

"Do you really think they can do all this at school?" asked Matt. "I mean, I hope they do—it's much more fun than lessons. But can you imagine Mrs Abbott feeding kids?"

"Or Mr Watts mucking out the pig shed!" said Stephen. "No. Mr Fox might be all right, though. I think he keeps some animals."

"Don't know about Mr Potter," said Matt.

"Oh, useless, I should think," said Stephen. "I quite like him, but he looks in such a muddle all the time."

"I don't think I even like him," said Matt. "Not since this morning, anyway."

After tea Mr and Mrs Chuff set off in the car to pick up Matt's mother and go to the meeting. Stephen and Matt decided to do their Maths homework, each of them glad of the other's help, and George sat sprawled in an armchair in front of the television.

"I'm not stopping in all night to look after you two," he said over his shoulder to his younger brother.

"Good," said Stephen.

After a pause, George added, "Don't know why you bother doing that Maths. You'll never need it when you leave school."

"*I* might not want to look after pigs," said Stephen.

"I won't look after pigs all my life," said George. "It's just a way to earn some money for now."

"What are you going to do, then?" asked Matt.

"I'm building up a motor bikes business," said George. "Repairs and servicing. Later on I'll get into sales. There's a terrific demand."

"You'll need your Maths then," said Stephen. "Count up your pound notes!"

"Nobody counts these days," said George. "Got calculators, haven't we?"

"There's VAT and all that," argued Stephen.

"Calculators do percentages, twit," said George.

The sudden wailing blast of a fire engine's siren interrupted the argument. All three boys rushed to the window and stared out as the fire engine tore past, followed after a few moments by another one.

"Ollie strikes again!" said Stephen, grinning. Matt pretended to hit him and Stephen said, "All right! I didn't mean it."

"Kevin said Gremmit's yard would go up," said Matt, worried. "Do you suppose that's what it is?"

"Too soon," scoffed Stephen. "They're not that stupid. I mean, if you're right and they *are* going to start a fire and blame it on Ollie, it's a bit obvious, isn't it? You can't go round saying, watch out for Gremmit's yard going up in smoke, and then set it alight the very same night."

"But supposing Ollie was there," said Matt, worried. "Everyone would think it was him, wouldn't they?"

George turned away from the window. "If he was there and this bloke you call Kevin Evans wasn't, then it probably *was* him," he pointed out. "Anyway, I think I'll go and see." He went into the hall and came back pushing his arms into his leather jacket. "You'll be O.K., won't you?"

"Of course we will," said Stephen. "I don't know why Mum worries."

"Neither do I," said George. He put on his crash helmet and did up the strap then went out, pulling on his gloves. His bike stood outside the front gate and he kicked it into action and rode off.

"It's years before I can have a bike," said Stephen gloomily. Then he brightened a little and added, "Still, I can do the same as George did—buy a wrecked one and rebuild it slowly so I can ride it round here. There's nothing to stop you riding on private property before you're sixteen."

"No, I suppose not," said Matt, who had never thought of it. "You're lucky having a place like this."

"It's great, really," agreed Stephen. "It's an awful lot of hard work, though. Mum thinks it's a laugh, the school doing this self-sufficiency thing. They don't know anything about it!"

"I suppose that's why they're having the meeting," said Matt. "So people like your mum can tell them how to do it."

"We've got enough to do on our own place," said Stephen. "Come on—let's finish this grotty Maths."

It was quite late when Mr and Mrs Chuff and Mrs Aiken came back.

"Where's George?" asked Stephen's mother.

"He went out," said Stephen. "We saw two fire engines go past and we wondered where they were going, so George said he'd have a look round."

"So much for your idea of a babysitter!" said Mr Chuff to his wife.

"We don't *need* a babysitter," said Stephen indignantly. "How often do I have to tell you?"

"I know you don't," agreed his mother. "But after all these years—"

"You get into the habit, don't you?" said Matt's mother.

"She won't even let me go to the boating pool to fly a model seaplane," said Matt gloomily. "Not that I've *got* a model seaplane, but there's no point in even *wanting* one."

His mother laughed. "Come on," she said. "We'd better be getting home, if Mr Chuff is going to be kind enough to give us a lift."

"Alan," corrected Mr Chuff. "Can't be doing with this Mr and Mrs bit. Stay and have some coffee—it's Saturday tomorrow. The kids don't have to go to school.".

"And I don't have to go to work," said Matt's mother. "Coffee would be lovely. My name's Ann, by the way."

"And I'm Barbara," said Mrs Chuff, going into the kitchen.

"What was the meeting like?" asked Matt.

Alan Chuff laughed. "I don't know how they're going to get on. None of them know the first thing about it. They're all dead keen, though. And Barbara's got herself on the committee. If I know her, she'll fetch up doing all the work."

"But what are they actually going to do?" asked Stephen.

"Michael North's going to spray the bit he ploughed for them, and harrow it," said Alan. "Make them a proper seed bed."

"I said I'd help plant seeds," said Ann, "So they'll probably *never* grow! I do like gardening, though," she added. "As soon as the builder's finished I'm going to tackle ours."

"What about animals?" asked Matt.

"Several people have promised chickens," said his mother. "And Mr Fox says we can start building a poultry house first thing Monday morning."

"The main thing they need is money," said Alan. "They'll have to buy things like breeze blocks if they want to keep pigs—timber's no good."

"Why not?" asked Matt.

"They tear it to bits," explained Stephen. "They'll be all right for weeks, then suddenly they feel a bit bored one day and start biting at the wood and the next thing you know, they've ripped a great hole in the wall. And once they've been out, they're much harder to keep in."

Matt nodded. "They would be," he said. He seemed to have learned a lot about pigs this evening. "Danny says they ought to play bingo."

"The pigs?" asked Stephen.

"No, stupid, the parents."

"Yes, they're going to do that next week," said Matt's mother. "And they're going to have a Summer Fair a bit later on, with lots of produce stalls and a Grand Auction Sale."

"They've left it terribly late," said Barbara Chuff, coming in with a tray of coffee. "A proper Fair takes months to organise. The Grand Auction Sale is a good idea, though. We'll sell anything for anyone, and the school keeps a quarter of whatever the article makes."

"If anything, that is!" said her husband, grinning.

Matt's mother stirred her coffee. Then she said, "I met a teacher called Mrs Abbott this evening."

Matt groaned.

"She seems to think you're getting into bad company," his mother went on. "But I couldn't get her to say who she meant. You go around with Danny Williams mostly, don't you? And he seems a nice little lad. Awfully scruffy, but nice."

"He's all right," said Matt. "And there's Bill North and Michael Chalmers sometimes and Peter Box—he's a bit thick but he's O.K. And then there's Rachel and Sue. And Felicity, I suppose. That's our lot."

"And me," said Stephen.

"I expect it's you she's thinking of," said his mother cheerfully. "Leading Matt astray."

"That'll be it," said Matt lightly. "Dreadful Stephen Chuff." He and Stephen glanced at each other briefly, both knowing full well who Mrs Abbott was referring to.

"Joking apart," said Ann Aiken, "I'd like to know what she meant. I do feel a bit worried, Matt."

To Matt's relief, the conversation was interrupted by the sound of George's motor bike roaring up to the front gate.

"Why do bike boys always have to rev their engines several times before switching them off?" asked Barbara fretfully. "It's a good thing we haven't got any close neighbours, otherwise they'd be complaining."

George came in and put his crash helmet on the table among the coffee cups. "Guess what?" he said. "It wasn't the builder's yard—it was the youth club."

"What are you on about?" asked his father.

"The fire. These two thought it might be Les Gremmit's yard because some kids at school have been saying Ollie was going to burn it down. But he wasn't at the yard tonight. He was at the youth club. Chantry. And guess what got burnt down? The youth club did."

"Was it actually burnt right down?"

"Did you see it?"

"Was Kevin there?"

"Did you see Ollie?"

They were all talking at once. "Shut up a minute!" George shouted. "I'm telling you, aren't I? The fire brigade was still there when I turned up, but the fire was more or less out. It had started in the basement, in some old curtains and things they'd got stored there."

"Was Kevin there?" asked Matt again. "Kevin Evans?"

"No, he wasn't," said George. "But Ollie was."

Matt felt his face redden, and his mother looked at him sharply. "Who's Ollie?" she asked.

"He's the assistant caretaker at school," Barbara told her. "Rather an odd sort of kid. Mr Hazzard's been very good to him and he's much better than he used to be but he's—well—a bit of a rough diamond."

"What *happened*?" Matt asked George, agonised. "Was Kevin there earlier? Did the police come?"

"I don't know about Kevin," said George. "Wouldn't know him if I saw him. But the others said he hadn't been there at all. The police were there, yes. That's why I've been so long. They wouldn't let anyone go until they'd taken their names and asked a whole lot of questions."

"I don't understand about all this," said Ann Aiken. "Is this Ollie person the bad company Mrs Abbott was talking about? What have you been up to, Matt?"

"I haven't been up to *anything*," said Matt. "But the way people are going on at me, I might just as well have been."

"Oh—wait a minute," said his mother, remembering something. "Wasn't it Ollie who rescued you when you were getting beaten up by those big boys the other day?"

"Yes," said Matt. "And he's all right. I don't care what anyone says."

Ann stared at her son, frowning. "I think I'd better write to Mr Potter," she said. "Perhaps he can sort it out."

"*Please*, Mum, don't do that," begged Matt. "Mr Potter doesn't like Ollie either. Just don't do *anything*. I told you before, it just makes things worse."

"He's probably right," said Alan Chuff, nodding at Matt. "We never found that writing notes did much good when George was at school, did we, Barbara? It only makes them think you're troublesome parents. Of course, it may be different now Mr Hazzard's there. He seems pretty reasonable."

"And it's different now George *isn't* there!" put in Stephen. "They've never complained about me, have they?"

"*There's* a good little boy," said George.

"You've only been there two terms," said Alan to his younger son. "I should jolly well hope they haven't complained. Not yet!"

Matt, still brooding darkly, did not laugh, and his mother glanced at him anxiously. "I think we'd better go home," she said.

Automatically, Matt got to his feet. Sticking up for Ollie seemed to be landing him in a load of trouble. And what if it turned out after all that he was wrong? What if Ollie *was* the firebug? Gloomily, he followed his mother out to the car.

CHAPTER 7

Rachel's Sale

"Matt," his mother called up the stairs the next morning, "there's two girls here called Rachel Greenberg and Sue Eames, and Rachel's mother. About a Bring and Buy sale. Do get up!"

"Oh. All right," said Matt. He had not been asleep exactly but it was nice just lying there. He pulled on his jeans and a T-shirt and went downstairs. His mother was making coffee and Sue was helpfully getting mugs out of the cupboard. Rachel was looking busy with a pencil in her hand and sheets of paper with lists written on them spread about on the table. Her mother, whom Matt had never met, was staring round the kitchen with interest. She had curly dark hair like Rachel's and wore a sleeveless dress over a faded Indian shirt.

"Hello," she said as Matt came in. "I'm Rachel's mum. Sorry if we got you out of bed."

"It's all right," said Matt, embarrassed.

"Coffee," said his mother, putting mugs on the table. "Do you want some, Matt?"

"No, thanks" said Matt. "I'll just have some corn flakes."

"What are you bringing to the sale?" asked Rachel.

"Let him have his corn flakes first," advised her mother. "Never ask men questions when they've just got out of bed."

Rachel sighed. "Waiting for people is so boring," she complained. "And I've got so much to do. Oh, Matt—guess what? The local paper rang up and said they'd heard about my sale. They're coming to take pictures this afternoon! Isn't that great!"

"How did they know about it?" asked Matt.

"The reporter said she went to the meeting at the school last night, and the headmaster mentioned my sale—wasn't it nice of him? I do think Mr Hazzard is sweet."

"I know," said Matt. "You seem to be completely nuts about teachers. You even like Mr Potter."

"Oh, he's *lovely*!" said Rachel. "I do hope he's coming to my sale."

"He won't dare miss it," said Sue, helping herself to another biscuit. "He's scared to death of you, Rachel."

"Don't be silly" said Rachel. "Of course he's not. But I shall be cross if he doesn't come. Are you feeling better now, Matt?"

"I'm all right," said Matt cautiously.

"Good," said Rachel. "Then what are you going to do?"

"I don't know," said Matt, wondering what Rachel had in mind.

"I really *love* this cottage," Rachel's mother said to Ann Aiken. "It's got the makings of something absolutely beautiful. What are you going to do with it?"

"Just the bare essentials at the moment," said Ann. "Mr Gremmit's doing the roof."

"We must have a get-together," said Mrs Greenberg. "I've got lots of ideas."

"Do stop talking about houses, Mum," said Rachel. "Matt, I think you'd better come with us. We're going to knock on doors and ask for things to sell. I haven't got nearly enough."

"I was going to see Danny this morning," said Matt, wildly inventing an excuse.

"We'll take him along as well," said Rachel firmly. She turned to Ann and added, "You're coming to my sale, aren't you, Mrs Aiken? It doesn't matter what you bring. A tin of beans will do, as long as it's something. You know where we live, don't you? Just across the Green. You can't mistake it—I'm putting a great big notice outside."

"Well, I suppose—er—yes," said Ann rather faintly.

"Good," said Rachel. She gathered up her lists and stood up. "We'd better be off, then."

Weakly, Matt allowed himself to be shepherded out. Danny was firmly collected from his house (he was still in bed, too) and they all set off for Flaxton in Mrs Greenberg's big estate car.

"Did you hear about the youth club?" Matt asked Danny.

"No. What?"

"There was a fire there last night."

"*No*!" Danny was impressed. "Was it burned right down?"

"I don't think so," said Matt. "I was at Stephen's and George went out on his bike to see where the fire engines were going. He said the fire started in the cellar."

"Just the sort of place someone *would* start a fire," said Danny.

"Was Ollie there?" asked Rachel.

"Yes," said Matt reluctantly.

"Oh," said Rachel. Then she added quickly, "But lots of other people must have been there, too. Just because someone's there, it doesn't mean they started it."

"Of course not," agreed Sue. "In fact, anyone who started it would be jolly careful *not* to be there."

"That's sensible," said Mrs Greenberg. "Rachel, where do you want to start?"

"In a road where the houses are fairly close together," said Rachel promptly. "Otherwise we'll spend too much time walking from house to house."

"This do?" asked her mother, slowing down.

"Fine," said Rachel. "You stay in the car, Mum, and we can put anything we get in the back."

Matt began to panic. "What do we do?" he asked. "You can't just knock on the door and ask people to give you something."

"No," agreed Rachel. "Not just like that." She thought for a moment then said, "Perhaps we'd better call it a jumble sale. It isn't, but people understand what jumble is. Just say, 'I'm collecting jumble for Mill Green School's Self-Sufficiency project'."

"And then they'll shut the door," said Sue, grinning.

Mrs Greenberg said, "Oh, do go if you're going. I'm not sitting here using up expensive petrol while you talk about it."

"Right," said Rachel. "All out!"

With great trepidation, Matt approached his first house.

It wasn't as bad as he expected. Apart from one rather deaf

old gentleman who couldn't understand what 'self-sufficiency' meant, most people either said, 'No, sorry,' or went in and brought out a contribution. They collected quite a lot of old clothes, a garden trowel with a split handle, a cactus in a pot, an alarm clock without a bell and a large meat dish with a crack in it. "Do for feeding chickens,' the man had said. There was also a pile of old magazines, a box full of half-used tins of paint and a garden gnome.

"Was it worth it?" asked Mrs Greenberg rather disparagingly as she set off homewards.

"Of course it was," said Rachel stoutly. "Those tins of paint are in a lovely strong box. It's bound to be useful for something. And I'm sure someone will buy the rest of the stuff."

"Oh, yes?" said Matt. "Who's going to buy a garden gnome?"

"No need to knock us gnomes," said Danny.

"Lots of people *love* them," said Rachel. "Just you wait and see."

At half-past two Matt and his mother walked across the green to Rachel's house. There were several cars standing outside, and a large, untidy notice dangling from a tree announced, 'Sale today! Bring something, buy something. For Mill Green School'. Matt grinned as he noticed the improved spelling. Obviously Rachel had taken Mr Potter's words to heart.

Two women converging on the house stopped to look at the notice and one of them said, "Terrible, isn't it? Fancy a school having to raise money like that."

"Shows the kids appreciate it, though," said the other one. "I wouldn't have lifted a finger to help my school raise money. I hated the place."

Matt and his mother followed the two women in and Matt was amused to see the first one pounce immediately on the garden gnome. "There's a dear little chap!" she cried. "How much is this, love?"

"A pound," said Rachel.

"Oh," said the woman, dashed. "Not cheap, then."

"It's for the school," said Rachel, gazing at her earnestly.

"Well—I suppose it's a good cause," said the woman reluctantly, fishing in her handbag. "Here you are, dear."

"Thank you," said Rachel. She gave Matt a triumphant smile and said. "Told you!"

"I brought this Airfix model," said Matt, handing over a large aeroplane. "It's a Lancaster bomber."

"It's super!" said Rachel. "Aren't you clever!"

"I've brought you some tiles," said Matt's mother. "They're rather pretty ones—I found them in the shed when I was clearing out."

"Oh, they're lovely!" said Rachel. "I bet Mum could think of lots of ways you could use them in your house."

"There aren't enough to do anything with," said Ann. "I think there's only a dozen or so. But the pattern's rather nice. They're quite old."

"Super," said Rachel, taking them. "And thanks for the aeroplane, Matt. Now—you'd better go and buy something before it all goes. And Mum's serving tea in the garden. Do stay and have some."

Matt's mother bought a huge sweater which looked as if it had belonged to a man twice her size. "I can never find woollies long enough," she said. "This one will be lovely for gardening. I'll put a belt round it."

Mr Fox turned up and bought the trowel with the split handle. "Soon put a new handle on that," he said. "Then it'll do for the scheme."

"Is Mr Potter coming?" asked Rachel.

"I don't know," said Mr Fox. "I think he's got his mother-in-law staying this weekend."

"Oh, dear," said Rachel.

"You shouldn't have suggested a competition to guess his baby's weight," said Sue. "You've frightened him off."

Mr Gremmit arrived, looking amazingly clean and tidy in a check sports jacket and a tie, and without his hat. His wife was with him and she at once made a bee-line for the clothes, sorting through them expertly. "Working shirts, he wants," she said. "Can never get enough. And the shirts they sell these days are such skimpy little things, aren't they. Ah, here's a nice one."

"I think I'll have a cup of tea," said Mr Gremmit. He turned to Matt and added, "See if you can get Ollie to come and have a cuppa. He's out the front—wouldn't come in."

Matt ran round the side of the house and found Ollie leaning against the side of Mr Gremmit's van, kicking idly at a clump of grass growing between two paving stones.

"Hello!" said Matt.

Ollie glanced up and nodded. Then he went on kicking at the grass.

"Aren't you coming in?" asked Matt.

"No," said Ollie.

Matt did not know what to say next. He stared at Ollie's slouching figure with exasperated affection and suddenly said, "Well, why did you come if you're not coming in?"

"Les wanted me to help him move some doors," said Ollie. "Dropped in here on the way, didn't he? I wouldn't be here else."

"I didn't want to come either," admitted Matt. "But it's Rachel's sale and she's in my class. There's nothing I want to buy, though. I thought I'd get a chocolate biscuit. Would you like one?"

"Wouldn't mind," said Ollie. To Matt's surprise, he detached himself from the van and shambled across the grass at Matt's side, hands in pockets. Mrs Greenberg had set up a trestle table on the lawn behind the house and was dispensing tea. There were plates of cakes and scones and people stood about in groups, talking and licking sticky fingers. The French windows into the sitting room stood open and sale goods stood invitingly inside. Ollie glanced at them casually then more attentively. Matt bought two foil-wrapped chocolate biscuits and took them back to the French windows. "Here you are," he said, giving Ollie one.

"Ta." Ollie fished in his pocket.

"No, it's all right," said Matt.

"Oh. Cheers, then." Ollie took a bite of his biscuit and picked up the top one of the stack of tiles Matt's mother had brought. "I like these," he said.

"Do you? They came from our house," Matt told him.

"What do you want for them?" asked Ollie.

"I don't know—I'll ask Rachel," said Matt. He found Rachel trying to sell the tins of paint to Mr Gremmit, and asked her about the tiles.

"Two pounds," said Rachel. "They're cheap at that. Honestly, Mr Gremmit, they're lovely colours."

Matt went back to Ollie. "She says two pounds," he reported. Ollie peeled off two crumpled pound notes from a small roll he took from his pocket, gave them to Matt and picked up the stack of tiles.

"What are you going to do with them?" asked Matt.

"Make a coffee table," said Ollie. "It's Mrs Morecambe's birthday next week."

"Oh, yes," Matt remembered. "She was your house mother."

"That's right." Ollie took the tiles and set off towards the van.

"I'll come and open the door for you," said Matt.

Ollie arranged the tiles side by side on the floor of the van. "Look nice, don't they?" he said.

"Yes," agreed Matt. He glanced at the jumble of ropes and buckets and tools in the van and said, "Do you like helping Mr Gremmit?"

"'sall right," said Ollie. After a pause he added, "Better than the school job. Won't have that much longer, don't suppose."

"Why not?" asked Matt, surprised.

"All this scheme thing," said Ollie. "Won't need me. What with that and the fires, I don't suppose I'll get a job anywhere."

"Of course you will!" said Matt hotly. "But anyway, you won't have to look for another job. The fires are nothing to do with you—I know they're not. I keep telling everyone."

Ollie gave him a rather odd smile. "How do you know?" he asked.

"I just do," said Matt, trying to forget the doubts he had felt last night. "You wouldn't do anything like that."

Ollie's smile ripened into a short laugh. "I got one friend, then," he said.

Matt blushed. Mr Gremmit came round the side of the house with the box of paints, followed by his wife carrying a pile of old clothes.

"Ditch those paints when we get back to the yard, Ollie," said Mr Gremmit as he put them in the back of the van. "They're no good. Box'll come in handy for something, I expect."

"How much did Rachel charge you for those?" asked Matt.

"Fifty pence," said Mr Gremmit. "I must want my head read. Still, it's for the school." He turned to his wife. "You're going home with Eileen?"

"Yes, she'll give me a lift," said Mrs Gremmit. "We're going to do a bit of shopping in Flaxton. Don't put your mucky old doors on top of those clothes, will you?"

"No, dear," promised Mr Gremmit.

As the van pulled away Miss Harker arrived on a bicycle.

"Hello!" said Matt, surprised. "Have you come to the sale?"

"Yes," said Miss Harker rather breathlessly. "If there's anything left, that is. I meant to get here earlier but things went all wrong."

Things always went wrong for Miss Harker, Matt thought. "Rachel will be ever so pleased you've come," he said, leading the way into the house.

Rachel *was* pleased. "Isn't that lovely!" she said. "Would you like a cup of tea?"

"I'd love one," said Miss Harker. Rachel led her into the garden.

"Has it been a success?" asked Miss Harker, accepting a cup of tea from Mrs Greenberg.

"Oh, yes," said Rachel. "We've sold almost everything. Tea's five pence, by the way. And cakes are five pence, too. Biscuits what it says on the wrapper—we had to buy those, but Dad can get them wholesale."

Miss Harker produced ten pence and took a piece of cake.

"Here's two pounds from Ollie," said Matt, handing the notes to Rachel. "He bought the tiles."

"Did he?" said Miss Harker, interested. "What's he going to do with them?

"He's going to make a tile-topped coffee table to give to his house mother at the Children's Home," said Matt. "It's her birthday soon."

"*Really*?" Miss Harker gazed at him in astonishment. "But I thought he was supposed to be such a toughie?"

"Just because you're tough," Matt told her, "it doesn't mean you can't be a nice person."

She looked at him respectfully and said, "I do believe you're right."

"There's not much left to buy," said Rachel. "A few clothes and that pile of old magazines, and the cactus. Oh, and Matt's aeroplane."

"Can I have the cactus?" asked Miss Harker. "I've always rather liked them. They don't mind too much if I forget to water them. And I'd like the magazines if they're not too expensive. I had an idea about using them for lessons."

Danny arrived just in time to hear this remark. He grinned and said, "They'll make smashing paper darts!" He looked particularly dilapidated in an unravelling woolly and filthy jeans.

Rachel looked at him coldly and said, "If you can't say anything sensible, you'd better go home again. You've missed the sale, anyway."

"Just as well," said Danny, unrepentant. "I'm broke. Is Stephen here?"

"No," said Rachel.

"Neither's Felicity," put in Sue, "but she said they were going to see her Gran."

"Stephen's helping George with some mucking out on the farm," Matt remembered. "He earns quite a bit of pocket money doing that."

"Oh, yes," agreed Rachel. "So he said." She turned to Miss Harker and added, "If you'd like the magazines, Miss Harker, they're only twenty-five pence. And the same for the cactus. It's in a nice little pot."

"All right, Rachel," said Miss Harker, smiling. "That'll be fine." And she gave her fifty pence.

"Thanks," said Rachel. "Now there just Matt's plane and the old clothes. I know. Mr Fox!" she shouted, "Don't go! Do you want some nice clean rags for the workshop? Cheap!"

"Isn't she marvellous!" said Miss Harker. "I could never have done anything like that at her age."

"I couldn't do it *now*," said Matt's mother. "I'll stick to being a part-time librarian."

Rachel piled a heap of old clothes into Mr Fox's arms and relieved him of twenty pence, then came panting back triumphantly. "It's all gone!" she said. "Isn't that good! I thought we'd get left with some of it."

"There's still my aeroplane," said Matt, beginning to wish he had never brought it along.

"I can't think why that hasn't gone," said Rachel, staring thoughtfully at the remaining people. "Now, who looks a likely buyer?"

Mr Fox reappeared, escorting a blonde girl who carried a notebook, and a middle-aged man with a camera round his neck. "Angela Purling from the Star," he introduced them, "and the photographer."

"Oh!" said Rachel, disappointed, "Why have you come so late? Everything's sold."

"Never mind," said the reporter. "You can tell me all about it. Has this lady bought something?"

"Me? Oh, yes, lots of old magazines and a cactus," said Miss Harker.

"That'll do fine," said the photographer, unslinging his camera. "Now, if the little girl will be putting the cactus on top of the magazines . . . no, *you* hold the magazines, Miss—er—"

"Harker," said Rachel. "She's a teacher at my school."

"Oh, *is* she?" said Angela Purling, scribbling busily. "Even better."

"Let's have a smile, then," said the photographer. "And again. Now just one more."

The reporter looked up from her notebook, pencil poised. "It's Rachel—?"

"Greenberg," supplied Rachel. "And this is Sue Eames, who helped a lot, and the boy with the fair hair is Matt Aiken. And that's Danny Williams."

"And you first name, Miss Harker?" asked Angela.

"Lucy," said Miss Harker

The photographer packed up his camera and declined a cup of tea, saying that he had to rush off somewhere else. Suddenly he noticed Matt's aeroplane. "Is that for sale?" he asked.

"Fifty pence," said Rachel promptly. "Reduced."

"I'll take it," said the photographer, fishing in his pocket. "My little grandson will think it's marvellous. He's mad about planes. See you back at the office, Angela."

"Right," said Angela. And as the photographer departed, carrying Matt's plane very carefully, she accepted a cup of tea and began to ask Rachel a lot of questions about the Down-to-Earth scheme and about the sale.

"Fine," she said at last, putting her notebook away in her hessian bag. "We'll do a bit in Monday's paper. Oh—how much have you made?"

"Twenty-four pounds, eighty pence," said Rachel promptly. "If someone would give us twenty pence it would make it up to twenty-five pounds."

"I'll do that with pleasure," said Angela, fishing in her bag again. "I think it's a marvellous effort. Was it your school that had the fire scare the other day, by the way?"

"Yes," said Rachel eagerly. "We're all wondering what's going to happen next, aren't we, Sue? And poor old Ollie thinks everyone's got a down on him and—"

Matt frowned at her but Rachel told the reporter all about it. To his relief, however, Angela said, "I don't think this is the kind of story we can use. We have to be very careful about sticking to facts, you see. But if anything startling does happen, I'd love to know about it. Just ring the office and ask for me. There's an answering machine if it's outside office hours so I'll hear what you've said as soon as I come in, and ring you back."

"Lovely," said Rachel. And she saw the reporter out to her car, still chattering eagerly.

"Good thing that man bought my aeroplane," said Matt. "I thought I'd have to take it home again."

"Don't know what you see in those models," said Danny. "Waste of time."

"And what do you do with *your* time, then?" enquired Matt.

"Muck about, mostly," said Danny cheerfully.

Matt groaned, and went to look for his mother. He was beginning to feel that this afternoon had gone on quite long enough.

CHAPTER 8

Who is the Firebug?

During the following week the school seemed, Matt thought, to go absolutely mad. People turned up with the most amazing amounts of stuff, some of it useful but much of it sheer junk. There were rolls of rusty wire netting and several hanks of rope, a lot of rough-hewn bean poles with last year's bean stalks still attached, two old sinks and a boxful of empty jam jars as well as stacks of other miscellaneous stuff. Parents arrived with contributions for the Summer Fair, though most of it seemed to consist of things they didn't want, such as old clothes and leaky wellies. They brought things for the Grand Auction, too—furniture and crockery, an old fridge and a record player and a dart board. "It's going to be quite a big sale," Rachel said, impressed.

John Beasley lugged an ancient mattress into the classroom, explaining that his dad said there was nothing like an old mattress to make good compost. Mr Potter gazed at him doubtfully and said, "I hope you're not thinking of us as a rubbish tip, John."

Rachel had a moment of glory when her picture appeared in the local paper and Mr Hazzard thanked her in Assembly for her marvellous effort in raising twenty-five pounds for the scheme. Ollie, on the other hand, began to look more and more depressed. He slouched round the school glowering darkly at everyone, and even Matt felt rather nervous of speaking to him.

The games pavilion began to fill up with offerings of all kinds, including a trailer-load of straw contributed by Mr North, and squads of boys and girls were to be seen at all hours of the day, digging and raking and planting. There were endless debates on the size and shape of pig pens and the dimensions of rabbit hutches, and the blackboards in the metalwork room were covered with designs for troughs and hay racks. Mr Murdoch's woodwork room, on the other hand, continued to display exploded diagrams of dovetails and halving joints, for Mr Murdoch regarded the scheme as an interruption to the process of education.

Matt, in common with most of Mr Potter's class, was so busy that he hardly thought much about the question of Ollie and the fire. However, the legend, "Ollie is a firebug" appeared again and again, scrawled on lavatory walls, written on doors and desks and emblazoned hugely in spray-can letters on the side of Ollie's shed. When this happened, Matt went in search of Ollie during morning break, and found him weeding the flowerbed outside Mr Hazzard's office.

"Hello!" said Matt.

Ollie glanced up, but said nothing.

"Have you finished your coffee table yet?" asked Matt. "The one with the tiles on it?"

"No," said Ollie.

He went on jabbing at the weeds and Matt fidgeted uncomfortably. "I'm sorry about all these things they keep writing," he said after a pause.

"Why are *you* sorry?" asked Ollie truculently. "You didn't write them, did you?"

"No, of course I didn't," said Matt, nettled by this injustice. "I just wish there was something I could do to stop them, that's all."

"Well, there isn't," said Ollie. He stood up and added, "I don't know why you keep on about it. You keep hanging round me and making a fuss, and I don't want to talk about it. It just makes me feel worse, having someone going on all the time. So just shut up, right? Go on back to your friends." Then, relenting a little at the sight of Matt's crest-fallen face, he added, "Anyway, you don't want to get mixed up in it."

Mrs Abbott came round the corner of the building and Matt remembered with sinking heart that this was her duty day. And she had caught him talking to Ollie in an out-of-bounds place last week, too. Not to mention the note in her class about Gremmit's yard.

"Matthew Aiken, come here," she said.

Matt cast a glance of appeal at Ollie, but he busied himself with the weeds as though nothing else could possibly interest him.

"You seem determined to disobey me," said Mrs Abbott tightly, "so there is no point in talking to you any further. Go and stand outside Mr Hazzard's office."

There was no point in arguing. Matt stood with his back to the cream-painted wall and waited. He was not sure whether Mr Hazzard was in his office of not. Mrs Abbott, having seen Matt to his place by the door, had gone outside again, but Matt dared not go away. Either now or later on, Mrs Abbott would tell Mr Hazzard about Matt's misdeeds, and there would be a fearful row if he had not stayed where he was told. But it was woodwork next, and he didn't want to miss that because he was making a box. They were all making boxes because Mr Murdoch said it was important, and Matt wanted to get it finished. He frowned, thinking about it. An unfinished box was such a useless thing.

Mr Hazzard's door opened suddenly and the headmaster came out. He almost walked past Matt, then paused and said kindly, "Did you want to see me, Matthew?"

Matt blushed. "Mrs Abbott told me to stand here," he said.

"Oh." Mr Hazzard raised his eyebrows. "Why was that?"

"I was talking to Ollie," muttered Matt.

"Talking to *Ollie*," the Headmaster repeated, sounding surprised. "I think you'd better come in." He led the way back into his study and sat down behind his large desk. "And *where* were you talking to Ollie?" he enquired.

Matt nodded towards the window and said, "Out there, sir. Just by the flowerbed."

"Where you are not supposed to be. Were you rude to Mrs Abbott?"

"No, sir."

"Had you done anything to upset her before this?"

Matt blushed even more. "I was talking to Ollie last week," he admitted.

"Are you a friend of Ollie's?" asked Mr Hazzard.

"No," said Matt reluctantly. "I mean—I'm only in the first year."

"And he's grown up."

"Yes."

"But you like talking to him?"

"Yes."

There was a pause and Matt felt that he was expected to say something more. "Ollie's all right," he said. "There's all this stuff about him being a firebug, but he isn't."

"I'm glad to hear you say that," said Mr Hazzard. "We all need friends sometimes, you know, but we don't always find them where we are looking."

Matt wondered what he was talking about. "No, sir," he said.

"The only thing is, Matthew," the Headmaster went on, "I wouldn't like to see you getting into any kind of trouble. School rules are meant for you as well as for everyone else, you know. I'd like you to apologise to Mrs Abbott and promise me that you will stay in the right place in future."

"Yes, sir," said Matt.

Mr Hazzard stood up and walked round his desk. "You might like to know," he added, "that I don't think Ollie is a firebug, either." He opened the door and ushered Matt out before him. "Now, run along," he said.

Miss Harker had brought a pile of magazines to her R.E. lesson that afternoon, and a box of scissors and some glue.

"Are those the magazines you bought at my sale?" asked Rachel.

"Yes, they are," said Miss Harker. "I had an idea about them."

"Did you?" said Rachel, interested. "What is it?"

There was a lot of noise going on as usual. "I'll tell you in a moment," said Miss Harker to Rachel. "When everyone's quiet." She got some sheets of blank paper out of the cupboard and put them on her desk with the other things, then stood up straight and said, "Everyone quiet, please!"

Nobody took any notice. "Shut up!" Rachel shouted at them. "I want to know what her idea is."

There were several jeers but the noise abated a little. Matt turned round and said loudly, "Look, why don't you pack it in? We'll have Mr Watts in here in a minute, then we'll all get in a row again."

Pink-faced but determined, Miss Harker said, "I am not going to tell you anything at all until you stop talking. Completely."

"Good old Miss," said Rachel approvingly. Sue dug her in the ribs and said, "Shut up, Rachel."

Eventually, the class was fairly quiet and Miss Harker began, "People don't go to church nowadays as much as they used to. A lot of people never even think about it."

"I went to my cousin's wedding," said Felicity.

"Ssh!" said Rachel. "Go on, Miss."

"I'm not here to say whether going to church is a good thing or not," said Miss Harker. "But I do think it used to provide something which is difficult to find these days. It provided someone to talk to." A babble of disagreement broke out at once, but she held up her hand and waited until there was quiet again. "I know we've all got heaps of friends to talk to," she went on, "but if there is something really worrying you, *then* who do you talk to? You see, people used to put their worries into their prayers, so they were talking to God about them—or they believed they were—or they could talk to the priest or the vicar. Sometimes they could talk to their family doctor, but these days doctors never seem to have time to talk to anyone. So who do you talk to if you are really worried?"

"Your mum," said Stephen.

"Yes, but who does your mum talk to about *her* worries?" asked Miss Harker.

"Your dad," said John Beasley, amid giggles.

Matt wondered when Miss Harker was going to get round to the magazines and the scissors and glue. She was beginning to look a bit harrassed.

"Now, listen!" Miss Harker said loudly. When they were all paying some kind of attention she went on, "What I want you to do is look through these magazines and find something which is about people talking to each other about something that matters to them. It could be a worry or a problem—but it mustn't be just idle chatter. When you find something you think fits the bill, cut it out carefully and stick it on a sheet of paper—you can work in pairs, one sheet between two."

There were groans and several people said, "Don't understand." Peter Box said, "Boring!" and put his feet on the desk in front of him.

"Shall I give the paper out?" asked Rachel

"Yes, please," said Miss Harker.

Chaos broke out at once. Danny said to Matt, "She ought to do what Mr Pebblemarsh does, and get all the stuff given out before she tells us what to do with it."

There was a crash and a cry of "You stupid twit!" as a pot of glue smashed on the floor.

"Oh, dear," said Miss Harker.

"Shall I get some paper towels from the boys' toilet?" offered Matt.

"Yes, please," said Miss Harker.

Half way along the corridor, a thunderous shout stopped Matt in his tracks.

"*Aiken!* Where are you going?" It was Mr Watts.

Matt turned to face the senior master. "Miss Harker asked me to get some paper towels from the boys' toilet, sir," he explained. "Somebody spilt some glue."

"Oh, *did* they," said Mr Watts grimly. He took Matt by the shoulder and propelled him along the corridor ahead of him, back to Miss Harker's room. As he flung open the door, silence fell. After a brief glance, Mr Watts said to Matt, "Right. Go and get those towels." As Matt hurried away he could hear Mr Watts' voice raised in a loud, fluent tirade.

Matt pushed open the door of the boys' cloakroom—and gasped. Smoke came billowing out. On the floor, Matt saw an untidy pile of paper towels which were smouldering ominously. The roller towel had been pulled out of its white-painted casing and yards of it lay doubled again and again on top of the paper bonfire. It, too, was beginning to char, and Matt saw that the whole heap was about to burst into flames. He rushed back to the classroom, flung open the door and shouted, "Mr Watts, there's a fire in the boys' toilet!"

Mr Watts held up a finger to the breathless class and said, "Get on with your work—and nobody move." Then he hurried out with Matt, stopping to snatch a fire extinguisher from its bracket on the wall.

Flames were beginning to lick round the edges of the pile of towels. "Go and get the caretaker," Mr Watts told Matt. Then he thumped the fire extinguisher upside down on the floor and a jet of foam burst forth with frightening strength. "Go *on*!" shouted Mr Watts over his shoulder. Matt went.

He ran outside, making for the caretaker's house, and saw Ollie tending a bonfire of leaves. Matt rushed up to him, shouting as he approached, "Where's Mr Amos?"

"Out," said Ollie. He hurled some bits of old timber on the fire—and Matt noticed with a pang of horror that charred pieces of folded paper littered the fire's edge. It had been lit with paper towels. "What d'you want him for?" asked Ollie.

Matt pulled himself together. "There's a fire in the boys' toilet," he said. "Mr Watts is putting it out but he said I was to get Mr Amos."

"Which toilet?"

"Near the library."

Ollie started across the grass at a run.

The smoke had abated when Matt and Ollie reached the toilet, but there was a terrible mess. Foam and bits of blackened paper covered the floor and most of the walls. Mr Hazzard had arrived and stood talking to Mr Watts, who still held the empty fire extinguisher.

"Oh, good," said Mr Hazzard, seeing Ollie, "just the chap I wanted. Have you seen anyone mucking about in here today?"

"No, I haven't," said Ollie, looking worried.

"Have you been in here earlier?" asked Mr Hazzard. "To clean up or put new towels in or anything?"

There was a fractional pause before Ollie answered, "No, sir!" Mr Watts glanced at him sharply and raised his eyebrows, and Matt knew he did not believe Ollie's reply. Mr Hazzard looked troubled and Matt himself, remembering those charred pieces of paper towel surrounding the bonfire, wondered if Ollie had lied.

"You can go back to your class now, Matthew," said Mr Hazzard. "Thank you for reporting the fire so sensibly."

On his way out, Matt glanced anxiously at the headmaster's face. Had he remembered what he had told Matt earlier about not believing that Ollie was a firebug? Mr Hazzard's pre-occupied expression gave him no clue.

Mr Watts called after Matt's retreating figure, "Tell Miss Harker she'd better start packing things up now. It'll take some time to collect all that glue and stuff before the bell goes. I'll be in shortly."

"Yes, sir," said Matt.

Danny and the others were all agog to hear what had happened. Miss Harker's classroom was littered with cut-out magazine scraps and everyone looked very sticky. "Mr Watts said we ought to start packing up now," Matt reported.

"Thank you," said Miss Harker. She looked depressed.

Although the clearing up happened very half-heartedly, Miss Harker kept telling everyone to be quiet, so Matt's news had to wait until after the bell had gone. He told them all about it on the way out to the bus, and they all stared curiously across at Ollie's bonfire, which was now burning fiercely.

"Who says Ollie's not a firebug now?" gloated Kevin Evans. His friends laughed raucously and Paul Arcot said, "Couldn't be anyone else, could it?"

Suddenly Danny gripped Matt's arm. "Look!" he gasped. Mr Fox was running across to the bonfire and started trying to snatch bits of wood out of the blaze. Then he shook his hand hard as if he had picked up something hot, and turned away. He looked very angry. As he came past them on his way back to the school, Rachel said, "What's the matter, sir?"

"Some idiot has put a lot of good wood on the bonfire, that's what's the matter," said Mr Fox crossly. "Just because it had a few nails in it, there was no need to burn it. Mr Amos must have taken leave of his senses."

"Mr Amos was out this afternoon, sir," said Kevin helpfully. His friends snorted with amusement and Mr Fox frowned. "Are you sure?" he asked.

"That's what *he* says," Kevin reported, indicating Matt. "Mr Watts sent him to find Mr Amos but he was out. Ollie was here, though."

"Is that right, Matt?" demanded Mr Fox.

Matt nodded unhappily.

Mr Fox pursed his lips in a silent whistle then turned on his heel and went into the school.

"Oh, *nice* one!" crowed Micky Brent, thumping Kevin on the back.

"I don't know, Matt," said Stephen Chuff as they got into the bus. "Ollie does seem to be up to the neck in all this. Are you sure you're right about him?"

"Of course he is!" said Danny indignantly.

Matt went and sat down without answering. The fire in the boys' toilet must have been started during the first two lessons of the afternoon, when the fifth year boys, like everyone else, were safely in a classroom. So this time it *couldn't* have been them. And why, he thought miserably, *why* had Ollie lied?

CHAPTER 9

An Unexpected Visit

When Matt and the others got off the bus the next morning, Mr Fox was talking to Ollie outside the first year doorway. "For goodness' *sake*," he was saying, "can't you *see* the stuff's useful?"

"It's no good you getting on at me," Ollie retorted. "I'm supposed to keep the place tidy, right? Piles of muck everywhere, I'll get it in the neck from Mr Amos if I don't do something about it."

"Of course you won't," said Mr Fox angrily. "That's just ridiculous. You're not here to decide what to throw away and what to keep—you just do the jobs you're told to do, and leave it at that."

"Well, then, why don't you do *your* job?" shouted Ollie. "You're here to teach kids, not to boss me about. Everyone thinks they can boss me about these days. The kids do my job, their blooming parents come in here and put stuff all over the place—there's no point in me being here at all."

"Oh, don't be so childish, Ollie," said Mr Fox, losing his temper. "It's difficult enough trying to get something going without people being petty-minded about it."

"You can just get stuffed," said Ollie. "You and your bloody school. If you want to sack me, I'll save you the trouble. I'm going."

"And good riddance!" said Mr Fox rashly.

Ollie strode away, his fists clenched. Then he shouted over his shoulder, "I hope the whole place gets burned to the ground!"

"Gosh!" said Danny, wide-eyed.

Mr Fox turned sharply to his fascinated audience and said, "Get off to your classrooms, you lot. No need to stand about with your ears flapping." And he strode away in the direction of the staff room.

"I *say*!" said Sue Eames, "Wasn't he cross!"

Matt was looking wretched. "He shouldn't have said that to Ollie," he said.

"Oh, don't be daft, Matt," said Stephen. "Mr Fox was quite right. It's not Ollie's job to go round deciding what to put on a bonfire. And anyway, fancy *having* a bonfire when there's all this talk about a firebug. It shows he must like burning things, doesn't it?

"I expect Mr Amos told him to light a bonfire," said Matt stoutly. But he thought of the charred paper towels and wondered again whether his defence of Ollie was all a big mistake. "I do wish we knew," he said, "about this beastly fire thing."

Rachel looked at him sympathetically as they went into Mr Potter's room. "We really ought to find out," she said. "One way or the other. I'll think about it."

"Oh, big deal," said Matt sarcastically. "That's all we need." Then he relented and said, "Thanks all the same."

"Special assembly this morning!" announced Mr Potter. "Mr Hazzard wants to talk to the whole school, so we're all going to the sports barn."

"Sir, why didn't they build us a proper hall?" asked Peter Box. "We had one in our last school."

"I've no idea," said Mr Potter. "That's architects for you."

"I'd like to be an architect," said Danny.

"Get off," scoffed Matt. "You're too small to lift the bricks."

"Architects don't lift bricks," said Danny with dignity. "They just make plans showing the builders where to put them."

"You need to be good at Maths if you want to be an architect," said Mr Potter. "And Art. And History, I should think."

"Oh," said Danny. "Well, that lets me out. Perhaps I'll drive an ice cream van instead. If I can reach the pedals."

The sports barn was the only place large enough to accommodate the whole school. It had no windows because there was gymnastic apparatus on every side and one wall was made for climbing, with chunky bits of brick sticking out to provide footholds. The translucent roof gave the place a rather unearthly light and Matt always felt that it was rather like being in a huge spaceship.

Mrs Gipsum played a hymn and Mr Watts said a short prayer, then Mr Hazzard climbed on to a stack of benches so that everyone could see him.

"The reason for this assembly," he said, "is to make you all aware of something very unpleasant which is going on in our midst. I expect you know that there have been a couple of outbreaks of fire lately. None of them has caused very serious damage, but we have to face the fact that if this goes on, the results may be disastrous and possibly dangerous. I am not telling you this in order to frighten you, because there is nothing to be frightened of. At least, not yet. But I do need your help." He paused and gazed round at his attentive audience. "With the best will in the world," he went on, "the staff cannot know each and every one of you as well as you know each other. Now, if anyone is likely to hear a whisper about who is starting these fires, that person 'in the know' will be one of you rather than one of us. What I am saying is, for Heaven's sake, if you think you know who is responsible, *tell* us. I guarantee that we will take no action until we are absolutely sure we have found the right people." He paused again, then added, "Lastly, I would like you to remember that this is *your* school. It is up to you to try and protect it."

There was some shuffling and muttering, and Mr Hazzard waited for quiet. Then he went on, "Turning to a happier subject, our self-sufficiency scheme is going wonderfully well and I am most grateful to all our helpers. We need lots more things for the Grand Auction, so if there's anything your parents would like to sell, get them to bring it here. There's money in it for them, and for us as well." And he got down from his bench.

Mrs Gipsum played 'The Cornish Floral Dance' but there was so much talk that the piano could hardly be heard. Mr Watts silenced the classes nearest him, but even he could not quieten the whole school.

"I wonder what'll happen now?" said Danny as they went out. "Do you think anyone knows anything?"

"Nothing more than we do," said Matt gloomily. "And that's not much."

"You think it's Kevin Evans and that lot, don't you?" said Rachel. "So why not say so?"

Matt thought. "I don't *know* it's them," he said. "I'm pretty sure they've been writing all those notices about Ollie being a firebug, but that's different from saying they started the fires. They're not the only ones who are fed up with school. There's lots of them in the fifth year."

"They can't have started the one at the children's home," said Bill North.

"Or the one in the bog," put in Peter Box. "Not if they were in a lesson."

"Or the one at the youth club," said Stephen, "because they weren't there."

"They might have been," argued Matt. "They'd take care not to be there when it was discovered, wouldn't they?"

Debbie Smart, overhearing this, said, "Roger says Ollie hasn't been to the club since the fire. Not once."

"That doesn't prove he did it," said Matt obstinately. "But I can't prove that Kevin's mob did, either. And Mr Potter said about giving a dog a bad name."

"What does that mean?" asked Peter.

"He was talking about the fifth year," explained Matt. "Saying some of them got blamed for everything whether they'd done it or not. So I can't say anything to him about it."

"Of course you can," said Rachel.

Matt glanced at her darkly. Rachel could be very irritating sometimes. And anyway, if Kevin's lot found out that somebody had told on them, it wouldn't be Rachel they'd go looking for. It would be Matt.

That afternoon, a group of parents arrived in Mrs Chuff's van and started to build a chicken hut, watched gloomily by Mr Murdoch from the window of the woodwork room.

Matt laughed as he walked across the open space to the Drama Hall with the rest of his form.

"Poor old Mr Murdoch," he said. "He does hate hammers and nails."

"He'd like them using secret mitred dovetails!" said Danny, grinning.

"And the chickens would get their shed in a year's time," added Stephen, "if they were lucky!"

Rachel looked thoughtful and said, "My parents think that a lot of what we learn at school is no good. They say most of us aren't going to get jobs, because there won't *be* any jobs, so we ought to be learning things that we do just for the interest of them. Then we can go on doing them when we've left, and we won't get so bored on the dole."

"What *are* you on about, Rachel?" asked Stephen. "There's always heaps to do. Keep chickens, for a start."

"That's just what I mean!" said Rachel. "Why don't we have lessons in chicken shed building?"

"Teachers don't *know* about chicken sheds," said Matt. "They only know about schools."

Mrs Palgrave whisked past them with her long fair hair blowing out behind her and her arms full of books. "Come on, you lot!" she said, "Don't dawdle about—we've got heaps to do!" And she pushed open the door into the Drama Hall and went in.

"I hate Drama," said Danny. "I always get so dusty."

"Do you?" said Sue, interested. "Why?"

"Because I always end up on the floor, being a corpse," said Danny. "Or a dog."

"I expect she thinks you look longer when you're flat than you do when you're upright," said Matt, grinning.

"Well, at least I'm *something*," said Danny. "It's better than being just ordinary."

When Matt went home that evening, Mr Gremmit was packing things into his van. "Aren't you having any tea?" asked Matt, surprised.

"Cheeky," said the builder. "I don't spend all my time drinking tea, you know."

"Oh," said Matt. Then, realising that this was rude, he

added quickly, "I don't mean you do. It's just that I always come home at tea time."

"Young Ollie was in a right tizzy today," said Mr Gremmit, tacitly accepting Matt's apology. "Turned up at mine this morning in a heck of a stew."

"He had an awful row with Mr Fox," said Matt.

"So he said." Mr Gremmit hurled half a bag of cement into the back of his van and shut the doors. "He said he wasn't going back to the school. Told them to stuff their job, he said. I told him not to be so daft. I mean, he's got a roof over his head there, and Ernie Amos isn't a bad sort. But I couldn't do nothing with him."

"Isn't he ever coming back, then?" asked Matt.

"Oh, I expect he will when he's calmed down," said the builder. "He stayed at mine this morning. Finished off that coffee table he was making, with the tiles on top. Made a nice job of it, too. Then he asked if I'd give him a lift over to the children's home with it, because he couldn't take it on his motor bike—but I couldn't do that. Not if I was coming over here to get finished off. I mean, time's money."

"He made the coffee table for Mrs Morecambe," said Matt. "She was his house mother at the home."

"So he said," nodded Mr Gremmit. "But I got a living to make. Anyway, he went off on the bus with it. Middle of the day, there's not many people on the buses. He'll manage."

"Was he cross about you not taking him?" asked Matt.

"*I* don't know," said the builder, who obviously didn't mind very much whether Ollie was cross or not. "Better not say anything to me, had he? He doesn't want to lose two jobs in one day."

"No," said Matt. "I suppose not."

Mr Gremmit went round to the driver's door of his van and got in. "I've finished here now," he said, "so you can have your breakfast in peace tomorrow morning!"

Matt wasn't sure what he should say to this, so he just smiled. Mr Gremmit reached a grubby hand through the window and added, "I'll be off, then. Be good!"

"Goodbye," said Matt. He shook Mr Gremmit's hand and the builder drove away.

Indoors, the kitchen smelled pleasantly of cooking. Matt's mother was busy with a mop. "Hello," she said, "keep your feet off the floor."

Matt pretended to climb up the wall. "Sit on the table, you twit," said his mother, "just while I finish this. Such a relief not to have Mr Gremmit trailing mud and plaster dust all over the place. Had a nice day?"

"It was O.K." said Matt, perching obediently on the table. "Mrs Chuff came in with some of the other parents and they built a chicken shed. They've nearly got it finished."

"Really?" said his mother, impressed. "The Chuffs are marvellous, aren't they? Ever so efficient. Compared with them, I feel as if I can't do anything."

"You make super cakes," said Matt. He sniffed. "What's in the oven?"

"A fruit cake," said his mother. "And I made some scones and a couple of sponges. They're in the larder. I thought I might go to the bingo session at the school tonight—not that I like bingo, but it's a way of making some money for them and—"

"Of course you must go," said Matt. "You never go to anything."

"Could one of your friends come round, do you think?" Ann Aiken wrung the mop out in the sink and gazed at her son anxiously. "I don't like leaving you alone."

"I'll be all right," said Matt. "I keep telling you."

"Perhaps you could ring up Danny," his mother persisted.

"*Mum*!" Matt was exasperated. "I'll be *all right*!" He jumped off the table and looked in the larder. "Can I have a scone?"

"Put them on the table," said his mother. "I'll make some tea. Leave one of the sponges, though. I said I'd take a cake to bingo. They're having a little sale of produce."

"By the time they've finished," said Matt, "they'll be *rolling* in money."

Later that evening, Matt sat in front of the television, writing laboriously in a notebook leant against his knees. Mr Potter took them for English as well as being their form master, and he was keen on poetry. "Macavity, Macavity, a monster of depravity," Matt read aloud. He sighed, and his gaze wandered back to the doings of a corrupt American policeman on the screen. Macavity had seemed quite funny when Mr Potter had first read it out, but it didn't seem so funny now. And writing about it was no joke at all because Matt kept forgetting what half the words meant. "Levitation," he muttered, reaching for his dictionary.

At that moment, somebody knocked at the door.

Matt stiffened. His mother's last words to him before leaving him alone were, "Don't open the door to any strangers."

But how could he find out who was at the door without opening it? And, having opened it, how could he keep out a stranger who wanted to come in? What's more, he told himself as he got up and walked across the room, anyone they knew would have come to the back door. So it *must* be a stranger.

The front door was stiff from disuse and Matt had to jerk it hard to get it open. Outside, it was almost dark and the person who had knocked at the door had retreated into the shadow of the unkempt honeysuckle bush.

"Who's there?" asked Matt nervously.

Without answering, the figure stepped into the light. It was Ollie Withett.

Matt gazed at him without speaking, feeling an odd mixture of happiness and fear. Was Ollie still angry? Why had he come here?

"I thought this must be your house," said Ollie. "Les hasn't moved his notice."

Matt looked. Sure enough, the black silhouette of Mr Gremmit's board was still visible in the garden.

"Can I come in?" asked Ollie.

"Yes, of course," said Matt, blushing. He should have asked him in straight away.

Ollie looked very big inside the house, perhaps because he wore a square-shouldered navy blue donkey jacket—or perhaps because Matt had never seen him in an ordinary room before.

"I brought you this," said Ollie. He took a narrow box out

of his jacket pocket and gave it to Matt. It was a balsa wood model kit.

"A Spitfire!" said Matt. "Oh, great!"

"It's not exactly a present," said Ollie. "Someone gave it to a kid at the home I was at—you know, I told you."

Matt nodded.

"But this kid can't make it up," Ollie went on. "He's a spastic, and his hands don't work properly. It was a stupid thing to give him, but he likes aeroplanes and this woman looked at the picture on the box and thought it would be O.K. Mrs Morecambe asked me if I'd make it up for the kid and I said I would. But you'd do it better than me. I've got such dirty great fingers." He looked at his big hands ruefully then added, "You don't mind, do you? Not having the plane to keep, I mean."

"Of course I don't mind," said Matt. "I never know what to do with them when I've made them, anyway. One day I'd like to make a seaplane that really flies but this kind without engines just hang around until they get dusty and bits start dropping off. That's why I gave that Lancaster to Rachel's sale. The fun's in making them.""

"That's O.K., then," said Ollie. He moved towards the door.

"Don't go," said Matt impulsively. "I mean—would you like some coffee or something?"

Ollie hesitated. "I wouldn't mind," he said. "What about your mum and dad, though? Would they—"

"I haven't got a dad," interrupted Matt. "He and mum split up ages ago. And mum's out tonight. She's gone to bingo at the school."

"Oh," said Ollie. "So you're all alone." He sat down on the arm of a chair, hands in his jacket pockets.

"I'll make some coffee," said Matt, feeling rather pleased that he was in sole charge of the house. It was much more grown up than having his mother there.

Ollie ambled out into the kitchen behind Matt and watched as he put the kettle on. "Mrs Morecamble liked her table," he said.

"Did she? That's good. I bet it looked super," said Matt.

"Les said it was O.K.," said Ollie.

There was a pause. Matt longed to talk to Ollie about the fire, but could not find a way to raise the subject. He made two mugs of coffee and said, "Would you like a bit of mum's cake?"

"Don't mind," said Ollie. Matt got out the fruit cake and the remains of the sponge and cut a slice of each. "We may as well eat it in here," he said. "I always spill things if I carry them into the other room."

"M'm," said Ollie, munching. "Good cake. You're lucky, having a mum."

This was the kind of remark which would have made Matt's friends at school tuck imaginary violins under their chins and play a weepy tune, but Ollie spoke in a matter-of-fact sort of way which did not invite pity.

"I thought Mr Fox made a silly fuss about that old wood," plunged Matt.

Ollie scowled and went on eating.

"I don't think you ought to leave just because of that, though," Matt ploughed on. "I mean, you won't have anywhere to live or anything. And if you leave they'll all say it proves you started the fires."

Ollie shot him a narrow glance from the black-lashed eyes which always startled Matt with their intense blueness. "What if they do?" he said. "I know I didn't, but I can't prove it."

"You might be able to if you stay there," insisted Matt. "They'll go on trying to blame it on you, and sooner or later they'll make a mistake, and get caught themselves. Bound to."

"Huh. Some hopes," said Ollie. Then he brightened up. "I'm in the clear about the one at the children's home, though. Mrs Morecambe says they traced a fault in the wiring."

"Oh, *good*," said Matt, relieved. Then he remembered something. "Mr Hazzard knows you're all right. He said so."

"Did he?" Ollie sounded surprised. "When?"

"Yesterday morning, when Mrs Abbott sent me to his office. You know, when I was talking to you."

"Silly cow," said Ollie.

"And he was very nice about it. He said I had to apologise to Mrs Abbott, though."

"And have you?" asked Ollie.

"Yes, I saw her this morning. She said, 'I will accept your apology, Matthew, but don't let it happen again.'"

"She would," said Ollie. "Why did he tell you it wasn't me, though? What did he say?"

"I said you were O.K.," said Matt. "And he said, 'I don't believe Ollie is a firebug either.' But then I had to go out."

"He's probably changed his mind by now," said Ollie gloomily. "After the fire in the bog. I wish I knew who'd done it. I'd kill him."

"Just as well you don't, then," said Matt. He thought, and added, "Who do you think it was?"

"I *think* it was those kids in the fifth year," said Ollie. "They've been a bloody nuisance for a long time. But I can't prove it. I wonder if they were in that bog after dinner time. I emptied the bin in there at about two o'clock, and there was no fire then."

"*Did* you?" Matt stared at him, his face flushing with excitement. "So *that's* why your bonfire had paper towels in it!"

Ollie stared back, frowning. "You were worried about that," he said. "Weren't you?"

"No, I was sure you didn't—"

"*Weren't* you?"

"I knew there must be a good reason," Matt insisted, his face now a fiery red. "I *wasn't* worried—honest!"

Ollie suddenly laughed. "You're a good kid," he said.

"But, Ollie," Matt said anxiously, "if you were in that loo at two o'clock, and nothing was wrong then, it makes it much easier to find out who did it. So why didn't you tell Mr Hazzard?"

Ollie sat back from the table and pushed his hands into his pockets again. "Daren't," he said. "If anyone thinks I was the last person in there before the fire started, they'll put me in the nick. It wouldn't be the first time."

"But you must tell them," Matt insisted. "Mr Hazzard's all right—he'll believe you."

"I'll tell him one of these days," said Ollie. "Perhaps."

CHAPTER 10

The Plan

Matt's mother came home very late. Ollie had departed some time earlier, admitting rather sheepishly that he was going to collect his bike from Gremmit's and then going back to the caretaker's house at school because he had nowhere else to sleep. Matt had washed up the plates and coffee cups and finished off his English homework, then, ages later than he had promised, he went to bed. He was almost asleep when a car drew up outside and cheerful voices called, "Good night, Ann! See you again soon!" Matt thought he would get up and ask his mother how the evening went, but suddenly he felt very warm and drowsy . . .

He overslept the next morning.

"Did you stay up late last night?" asked his mother as Matt rushed into the kitchen with uncombed hair and grabbed a piece of now-cold toast. "That's three times I've called you."

"No," lied Matt, struggling into his anorak with his toast held between his teeth. He grabbed his sports bag with his homework books in it, took a bite out of the toast and said indistinctly, "See you." Then he ran all the way to the bus stop.

"Just made it," said Danny. The bus was coming down the road. "Heard about Gremmit's?"

Matt stared at him, panting. He was still holding the piece of toast. "What?" he asked.

"Went up in flames last night."

"No!"

"It did. It was on the news this morning. Didn't you hear it?"

"Don't have it on in the mornings. Overslept, anyway. Hey—it wasn't Ollie! He was at my house."

"*Ollie* was?"

"Yes."

The bus pulled up and they all got in. The fifth year boys were digging each other in the ribs and shaking clasped hands above their heads like victorious football fans.

"But when?" demanded Danny. "When was Ollie at yours?"

"He came nearly at the end of that film—about the policeman who took drugs," said Matt. He was still out of breath.

"About quarter to nine," translated Danny.

"And he stayed about an hour—perhaps a bit more. He brought a model for me to do." Matt started to explain but Danny interrupted to say, "I think the fire started earlier than that. I heard the fire engines go past at about eight o'clock."

"I didn't hear them," said Matt.

"No. Well, you wouldn't," Danny pointed out. "If they were going to Gremmit's, they'd pass my house and go out along the Withersett road."

"I wish I hadn't brought this toast," said Matt. "I don't feel like eating it now."

"Can I have it?' asked Danny.

"You're welcome," said Matt. He stared out of the window as Danny munched beside him and the fifth year boys chanted and cheered in the back. He had felt so happy last night. And now things were worse than ever.

The school seemed to be crawling with policemen. Several police vans and cars stood in the bus parking place, and the fifth year boys stopped cheering as they got out of the bus under the eagle eye of a large police sergeant. Matt saw Mr Amos standing at the gate of his house and rushed over to him.

"Is Ollie here?" he asked.

"No, Ollie's not," said Mr Amos shortly.

"But where is he?" asked Matt, distraught.

"Down the nick," said Mr Amos. "They picked him up last night, at Gremmit's yard."

"But he was at my house!" protested Matt. "He only went to get his bike from the yard!"

"That's *his* story," said Mr Amos grimly. "Walked in as bold as brass. Fire was out by that time, of course, so I suppose he didn't expect there'd be anyone about. But the police aren't that daft. They had a van down the side street opposite."

Matt was almost in tears. "It's all wrong," he said. "He didn't do it. I know he didn't."

"You'd best get off to your classroom or you'll be in trouble and all," said Mr Amos. And as Matt turned away dispiritedly the caretaker called after him, "And be careful who you make friends with in future!"

With considerable self-control, Matt managed not to turn round and tell Mr Amos what he thought of him, but the unspoken words rang loudly in his mind as he stumped along with his hands thrust deeply into his pockets and his sports bag bumping against his legs at every step. With his head down, staring at the muddy, monotonous grass, he did not see anyone coming until a voice spoke to him at close quarters.

"Matthew. Just the chap I want to see."

It was Mr Hazzard.

"Come into my office for a minute," he went on. "I take it you've heard the bad news about last night?"

"Yes, sir," said Matt.

The Headmaster led the way back to the building and stopped to wipe his shoes on the big doormat inside the main entrance. "I get into terrible trouble with the cleaners if I tread mud into the office," he said. Matt smiled politely as he wiped his own shoes, but could find nothing cheerful to say in response.

Mr Hazzard sat down behind his desk and pulled up a chair for Matt to sit beside him.

"The police tell me Ollie was at your house last night," he said. "Is that right?"

"Yes, sir," said Matt.

"Had he ever been to see you before?"

"No, sir," And Matt explained exactly why Ollie had come.

The headmaster listened patiently, then nodded. "What a

nice thing to do, making the aeroplane for the little lad," he said. "And what time did Ollie arrive?"

"About quarter to nine," said Matt. "He'd just come from the children's home on the bus. Or perhaps a bit earlier. I was finishing my English homework."

But Mr Hazzard's mind was not on homework. "How far is it from your house to Mr Gremmit's yard? he asked. "Walking that is. How long would it take?"

Matt thought. "About twenty minutes," he said. "You can go along the field track, you see. It's much further round by road."

Mr Hazzard fished on the shelf behind him and produced an Ordnance Survey map which he unfolded and spread on his desk. "Show me where you live," he said.

Matt pointed out his house and then, at Mr Hazzard's request, showed him where the children's home was, right out on the left-hand edge of the map, and the exact spot of Mr Gremmit's yard, to the right of Matt's house. The Headmaster nodded. He did not look happy.

"Ollie couldn't have done it, sir," said Matt earnestly. "Could he?"

"I hope not," said Mr Hazzard, frowning absently. "I really do hope not. Thanks for all your help, Matthew. You'd better run along to your class now."

"Yes, sir," said Matt. He went to the door slowly, thinking about the pattern of Ollie's movements the previous night and trying to understand why the headmaster looked so worried. Then he saw it. He turned and asked, "Sir—what time did Ollie leave the children's home?"

"He left at seven o'clock," said Mr Hazzard. He and Matt looked at each other, and the same dreadful understanding was written on both their faces. There had been enough time for Ollie to have visited Gremmit's yard before he arrived at Matt's house. He might have stayed on the bus all the way to the yard, then walked back to see Matt. In which case, there was only one explanation. He wanted to create an alibi.

"Oh, *there* you are," said Mr Potter crossly, getting his red pen out again to mark a line beside Matt's name on the register. "Where have you been?"

"I had to see Mr Hazzard," said Matt.

"Oh. Well, there's nothing I can say about that, is there?" said Mr Potter. "Collapse of stout party. What did he want you for?"

"It was about the fire last night," said Matt cautiously.

"Good God," said Mr Potter. "You didn't light it, did you?"

"No," said Matt. And he suddenly giggled because Mr Potter looked so pop-eyed. Everyone booed in a friendly way and said, "Yes, he's the one," and, "Search his pockets, sir—they're full of matches," and other things of that kind, and Matt felt a lot better.

"Look, Matt," said Mr Potter, "I don't know much about what's been going on, but it seems to have been a bit heavy—know what I mean? Quite a lot to cope with. So if I can help in any way, don't be afraid to give a shout. O.K.?"

Matt nodded. "O.K.," he said. "Thanks."

"There," said Rachel sentimentally. "I always said Mr Potter was lovely."

"I'm not lovely to everyone," said Mr Potter, trying to look fierce. "If I find out who's at the bottom of this fires thing, I won't be lovely at all. Matt, I gather you're not happy about some of our friends in the fifth year?"

Matt shot Rachel a suspicious glance but she quickly found something to say to Sue Eames and would not meet his eye.

"I can't prove anything, sir," he said carefully.

"There's been a lot of mucking about on the bus, hasn't there," said Mr Potter. "John Beasley, do be quiet. And I understand you reported three lads for smoking."

"I just told the driver their names," said Matt. "I didn't tell a teacher or anything."

The bell rang and everyone stood up. Mr Potter shrugged in exasperation and Matt heard him say, "There's too many lessons in this place and not enough bloody education." Matt grinned. "See you in English, sir," he said as he went out. Mr Potter nodded. He could not have made himself heard in the torrent of conversation.

Most of the girls chose to do Home Economics when the boys did Metalwork, but Rachel said she knew how to cook already but her mother couldn't teach her Metalwork. And Sue Eames came along to keep her company.

Matt put on his apron and waited for Rachel's dark, curly head to appear from the old shirt she was struggling into.

"Did you tell Mr Potter I thought it was Kevin Evans?" he demanded.

"Yes," said Rachel calmly, rolling up her sleeves.

"What did you do that for?" asked Matt. "You knew I didn't want to tell him."

"That's why I had to," said Rachel. "Teachers are only *people*, Matt. You mustn't be afraid of them."

"I'm not," said Matt. "But they're not as nice as you think. And I just wish you wouldn't keep minding everyone else's business, that's all."

"There's gratitude for you," said Sue Eames.

Mr Fox pushed the rotary blackboard up until his designs for a feeding trough came into view and called, "Bring your stools round here."

"I hope we can actually make something this week," said Stephen. "My dad would have knocked something up by now and had it in use."

"Well, we can't all be geniuses," said Danny.

"Knocking things up is all very well but it doesn't last," said Bill. "Might as well do the job properly in the first place."

"*Your* dad would just go down the road and buy it," retorted Stephen.

"Quiet!" shouted Mr Fox. When they were all listening he went on, "I've told you before, I don't like a lot of noise in the Metalwork shop. If you don't pay attention to what you're doing you'll hurt yourselves. So shut up. Right?"

"Right," said Rachel.

"Mr Fox is awful about talking, isn't he?" said Danny to Matt as they left the Metalwork shop at break time. "There's ever such a lot I wanted to say."

"Me, too," said Matt. "Mr Hazzard thinks there was time

for Ollie to have been to Gremmit's yard before he came t mine."

"But he *can't* think Ollie did it," said Danny. "Specially now it's proved he didn't start the one at the home."

"Mr Hazzard might not know that yet," said Matt fairly. "I ought to have told him. I didn't think."

"We've got to make a plan," said Rachel decisively.

"What sort of plan?" asked Matt.

"About Ollie, of course!" said Sue. "You can see nobody else is going to do anything?"

"What do you mean to do?" asked Matt nervously. "You're not going to storm the police station—"

"Oh, don't be *silly*, Matt!" said Rachel. "Getting Ollie out is no problem. I asked my dad. You just give the police some money and they let him out. It's called bail."

"But we haven't got any money," objected Danny.

"Oh, somebody else will do that," said Rachel impatiently. "Mr Hazzard or someone. No, I've thought it all out. What we've got to do is make the real firebug start another fire while Ollie is still in prison. That would *prove* it wasn't him."

"Oh, yes?" said Matt. "And how do we do that?"

"*I* don't know," said Rachel, spreading her hands. "That's why we need a plan."

They were still arguing about it fiercely when they had to go in for Mr Potter's English lesson, but some progress had been made. Matt had suggested that they needed an attractive target to put forward as a good place to start a fire, and Stephen had pointed out that the obvious place was the games pavilion with its accumulated store of goods for the Grand Auction. Ollie was well-known for his dislike of parents coming into the school and 'cluttering the place up' with their contributions; what's more, a lot of people had heard him shout at Mr Fox that he hoped the whole place would burn to the ground.

"It needs another special assembly," said Rachel. "If we could get Mr Hazzard to say that he was worried about the stuff stored in the games pavilion, and warn everyone that Ollie had been let out of prison, that ought to do it."

Matt shook his head. "I wouldn't," he said. "It would seem far too obvious. They'd never fall for it."

"Fall for what?" asked Mr Potter, coming in. A sudden hush fell and everyone looked at each other, wondering whether to include him or not.

"Well, come on," said Mr Potter. "You'll either have to tell me what you're up to or we'll get on with Old Possum's Book of Practical Cats."

"Tell him," said John Beasley gloomily. Everyone laughed, but still nobody said anything.

"The trouble is," said Rachel, "you're a teacher."

"Yes," agreed Mr Potter.

"Can't you imagine you're our uncle or something?" Sue suggested. "So we can talk to you properly."

Mr Potter pushed his hands through his hair unhappily. "I can see you're going to put me in a moral dilemma," he said. "I'd really much rather you didn't."

Everyone looked at each other, and somehow they all knew that they were not going to tell him.

"That's all right, then," said Rachel briskly. "On with the Practical Cats."

Amid groans, they started to get out their books. Rachel nudged Matt. "We'll keep spreading the rumour that Ollie is annoyed about the stuff in the pavilion," she whispered. "I've told lots of people already."

"But we can't do anything about keeping Ollie safe," objected Matt. Then he had an idea. "Unless I tell him about our rumours. If they let him out, that is."

"That's it!" said Rachel. There was too much general noise for Mr Potter to hear her. "Brilliant! Ollie can keep himself safe! You are clever, Matt!"

"You mean," said Sue, "Ollie mustn't go anywhere without making sure someone is watching him?"

"That's right," said Rachel. "Then nobody can blame him if a fire starts."

"Rachel, stop talking at *once*!" said Mr Potter crossly.

Rachel shot him a black look. "Fine sort of uncle *he'd* be," she muttered to Matt.

Matt grinned and shook his head. He could never quite

share Rachel's view of teachers as ordinary people. To him, teachers were always just teachers. Smothering a yawn, he turned to Macavity.

CHAPTER 11

Things Look Bad

On the bus that evening, Kevin Evans and the others sat in sulky silence, their feet propped on the back of the seats in front of them.

"Bloody coppers," said Kevin. "Nothing but flaming hassle all day." His injured innocence sounded, Matt thought, a bit too good to be true. Or was he imagining it?

"They must be thick in the head, I reckon," said Paul. "The one who was talking to me kept asking the same questions over and over again. Did I go to the youth club, did I know where Gremmit's yard was, where was I last night—"

"Same with me," agreed Micky Brent. "Asked me where I lived about fifteen times, and then about the youth club. Good thing we was all at yours last night, innit, Kev?"

Rachel suddenly glanced at Matt with a sparkling expression on her face which alarmed him. What was she going to do now? She knelt up on her seat so that she could see the boys in the back and said ingratiatingly, "Kevin?"

"Wotcher want?" scowled Kevin.

"I just wanted to say I'm sorry," said Rachel innocently. "I really thought it might have been you lot that started the fires because you wanted to get even with Ollie Withett. But I mean, after last night, it *must* have been him. So I just wanted to say I'm sorry. Forgive me?" Her face was sweetness itself, wide-eyed and appealing.

Kevin gave her an incredulous stare. Then he laughed. "Ain't she lovely?" he said. "What a *nice* girl!"

"Well," said Micky Brent virtuously. "I mean, we *didn't* start the fires, did we?"

"Of course we didn't," said Kevin. "We been saying so all day, haven't we?"

"Time somebody believed us," agreed Paul.

"Well," ended Rachel with a shy smile. "I just thought I'd say." And she sat down.

Sue's eyes were streaming with the tears of silent laughter. "You are awful, Rachel," she said.

"I just thought I'd say," repeated Rachel, still maintaining her pose of wide-eyed innocence. Then she, too, could not repress a giggle. She leaned across the gangway and whispered, "You have a go, too, Matt. Pretend you're awfully upset at finding out Ollie really did it. If they believe us they'll feel so safe, they're bound to go ahead and light another fire."

"If they lit one at all," said Danny.

"What if they don't believe us?" muttered Matt.

"Then you'll get beaten up again," said Rachel fiercely. "And serve you right. Don't you *dare* let me down."

Matt and Danny, Rachel and Sue all got out at the next stop and Matt, greatly daring, risked a mournful glance in Kevin's direction as he got up.

"What's the matter?" bawled Kevin. "Don't the sun shine out of Ollie's bum no more?"

"All right, so he's the firebug," Matt shouted back angrily. "You don't have to go on about it, do you?"

"Yes," chipped in Danny, "just because you didn't light the beastly fires, there's no need to be so snotty about it!"

Kevin and his friends fell about with laughter as Matt and the others shuffled glumly off the bus.

"Oh, marvellous!" gasped Sue when the bus had pulled away. "You were terrific, Danny! Mrs Palgrave would have been proud of you!"

"Well," said Danny modestly, "it's better than being a dog."

But Matt was not happy. Kevin and the others had sounded genuinely innocent. Could they really be pretending?

Matt came in through the back door to find Mr Gremmit sitting at the kitchen table with his mother.

"Hello," said the builder, stirring his tea. "Just came to collect my notice board. Always like to leave it a day or two, advertise a good job done."

"I was sorry to hear about your fire," said Matt. "Was it a bad one?"

"Tell you the truth," said Mr Gremmit confidentially, "I wasn't sorry to see most of it go. The new stuff was in the other building, see. It was a stack of old roofing felt that went up. It burns like fun anyway, and the fire officer said they'd poured creosote over it. Must have been a hell of a blaze. I lost a couple of good ladders and most of the fence, but it's all insured, of course."

"Who on earth can have done it?" wondered Matt's mother. "Was it that boy Ollie, do you think?"

Mr Gremmit shook his head. "Can't say," he said. "I was out at a darts match, see. We were playing away, over at the Six Bells in Flaxton, so I left early. Time I got back, it was all over and they'd got Ollie in the nick. I can't think it was him, though, somehow."

"Have you seen him since the fire?" asked Matt.

"No, I haven't," said the builder. "Mind you, it was only last night. And I've been that busy today, with the police in and out all the time, and the fire officer, and ringing up the insurance—"

"Such an awful thing to happen," said Matt's mother.

"Ollie came here," said Matt. "I didn't have time to tell you this morning, Mum."

"Did he?" said Ann. "So that's where all the cake went! I thought you couldn't have eaten all that. What time was he here, though, Matt? I mean, could he have—"

"Started the fire? Yes, they think he could," Matt admitted. "But I'm sure he didn't." He fetched the model aeroplane kit and told his mother why Ollie had come. She stared at the box in Matt's hands with a troubled expression and said, "He doesn't *sound* like the sort of boy who'd start a fire."

"He told the police he walked from the children's home to your house," said Mr Gremmit. "Well, I mean, that's a tidy step. If anyone was to walk all that way, it would take them the best part of two hours."

"But it's miles!" said Matt's mother. "He couldn't have walked that distance—nobody would."

"Ollie might do anything," said Matt. Then he realised what this could be taken to mean and added, "Anything a bit odd, that is. But he wouldn't start a fire."

"I hope not," said the builder. "Tell you the truth, I rather like the lad."

"So do I," said Matt.

On the following morning, the school had nearly as many parents in it as children. Several fathers were already busy in the garden and Mrs Chuff had arrived with a number of other people and two crates of chickens, which they were installing in the newly-finished pen.

"What sort of chickens are those?" asked Matt, looking at them through the bus window.

"Brown ones," said Danny.

"Stephen will know," said Rachel. "I expect he got a lift in his mother's car. He's not on the bus."

"They're Rhode Sussex," said Bill North. "Rhode Island Red crossed with Light Sussex. The big poultry people don't use them any more. Modern hybrids are—"

"Oh, shut up, Bill," said Matt. "We don't want one of your lectures."

"Boring," agreed Danny.

"Suit yourselves," said Bill, resigned. "*Be* ignorant."

"We'll ask you when we want to know," Rachel assured him. Then, surveying the scene, she added, "What's Felicity's dad doing?"

"Arguing with Mr Potter," said Sue.

"What's in that newspaper bundle he's got?" Matt wondered. "It's something green."

"Cabbage plants," said Bill, and added quickly, "*Boring*."

"Don't be like that," said Rachel. "Oh, I know! He'll be trying to drive a bargain with Mr Potter about how many cabbages he can have if he's allowed to put his plants in the school plot."

She was right. As they walked from the bus to the first year entrance, they heard Mr Potter saying, "I really can't enter into any hard-and-fast arrangement of that kind. Why don't you just put your plants in, and we'll talk about it later."

"I want to know *now*," objected Mr Banks.

Felicity joined the others and said, "Dad is awful. He's ever so keen on the scheme really, but he says he won't do it for nothing. He's on short time at the bacon factory and he seems ever so ratty."

Stephen came running over and said, "Tell Mr Potter I'm here—I'm just going to give them a hand unloading a corn bin."

"You don't *have* to do that," Rachel pointed out. "There's plenty of parents over there."

"I know," agreed Stephen, "but it's better than sitting in a classroom, isn't it?" And he ran off again.

"You are snooty sometimes, Rachel," said Matt, who was feeling irritable himself this morning. It was so awful, not knowing what to do about Ollie.

Rachel tossed her curly head and said, "Well—he's such a *kid*."

Then, coming round the side of a building with his wheelbarrow, looking as if nothing had happened, Matt saw Ollie.

"Look!" gasped Matt, "there's Ollie! They've let him out!" He ran across to try and talk to him but almost collided with Mr Potter, who had abandoned his conversation with Mr Banks and was returning rather crossly to the school.

"And where are *you* going?" he enquired, fielding Matt with an outstretched arm.

"See Ollie, sir," said Matt.

"No, you're not," said Mr Potter firmly. He turned Matt round and propelled him back towards the school. "You're going to go into the classroom with the others and behave like a normal, ordinary boy instead of playing at Emil and the Detectives."

"Oh, come on, sir," said Rachel, overhearing the last sentence as Mr Potter and Matt joined the rest of the group. "He's not playing at anything. Don't be so stuffy!"

Mr Potter turned pink. "There are times, Rachel," he said, "when I think you're just plain rude."

Sue sprang to her friend's defence. "She's not being rude, sir. She's just saying how things are. *We* wouldn't think it was rude if she said that to one of us, so why do you?"

Mr Potter ran his fingers through his hair. "Oh, *I* don't

know," he said irritably. "It just looks like being one of those thoroughly awful days."

"You can say that again," muttered Rachel darkly. "I've been called snooty *and* rude in the last five minutes, and the day hasn't even started yet."

Matt doodled inattentively on the cover of his music book while Mrs Gipsum was drawing a diagram on the blackboard showing how an orchestra was arranged. He had a vague impression of a fan-shape with a little box in the middle which was the conductor, but he was too busy thinking about Ollie to take much notice.

"And here," said Mrs Gipsum, pointing, "we have the woodwind section. Now, who can tell me some of the instruments we find among the woodwind?" A few hands went up, but her eye lit upon Matt's averted head. "Matthew Aiken?"

Matt was gazing out of the window and did not realise that he had been spoken to. Danny nudged him and he turned back to look at the teacher. "Yes?" he said.

Mrs Gipsum pursed her lips. She had frizzy permed hair which sat in a bouncy heap on her forehead and Matt always thought she looked like a poodle. "And what," she enquired, "is so fascinating outside?"

"Nothing," said Matt, blushing.

"I find it rather insulting," she went on, "that you find nothing so much more interesting than my lesson. Or perhaps you are so brilliant that there is no need for me to teach you at all. You *know* all the instruments in the woodwind section, do you?"

"No, miss," said Matt.

"Surely you know at least *one*?" persisted Mrs Gipsum.

"Trumpet," Matt guessed wildly. Everyone laughed.

"Trumpets are *brass*," said Mrs Gipsum heavily.

Rachel put her hand up again. "What is it, Rachel?" Mrs Gipsum asked.

"Clarinet," said Rachel, coming to Matt's rescue.

"Oboe," said Sue faithfully.

"That's better," said Mrs Gipsum, successfully diverted. Matt glanced at Danny and made a face, and Danny wrote on his music book, "Better wait till break," then rubbed it out.

It was Mr Potter's duty day and Matt watched carefully until he was out of the way before he went in search of Ollie. He looked in all the likely places but could find no sign of him. He was not sweeping the paths or mowing the grass and there was nothing left of the bonfire except ash and a few bits of charred wood. And at any minute the bell would go for lesson time again. Matt ran across the grass to Ollie's shed and banged on the closed door, but there was no answer. The bell rang in the school building and he turned away dispiritedly and retraced his steps towards the school. He had just reached the paved area when Ollie came out of the main door. Matt ran up to him. "I've been looking for you *everywhere*," he said.

"I was in the head's office," said Ollie. "What did you want?"

Everyone else had gone into the school.

"We're trying to get the fifth years to start another fire," said Matt quickly, "so they'll get caught. But you must keep out of the way so everyone knows it's not you. Stay with Mr Amos all the time or something."

Ollie frowned. "You want your head read," he said. "You can't get mixed up in this—and what's it all about, anyway? I don't get it. What are you on about?"

"I can't stop now," said Matt desperately. "Can I see you at dinner time?"

"No," said Ollie. "I got to go and see the social worker. He's coming over dinner time so he can see me and Mr Hazzard and Mr Amos all together. Mr Hazzard's got Mrs Amos cooking lunch for us."

Mr Potter came round the corner and put both hands to his head in a pantomime of desperation when he saw Matt. "Will you *please* get off to your lesson!" he almost shouted. "You seem to have completely taken leave of your senses, Matt. Who have you got next?"

"Mr Watts," said Matt.

"In that case," said Mr Potter, "you really *have* taken leave of your senses."

Matt grabbed his bag of books and fled.

The rest of the day dragged. Matt did not see Ollie at

dinner time or during the brief afternoon break, and got on the bus feeling very despondent. Mr Watts had given him such a terrible telling-off for arriving late that Matt was still smarting; and it looked as if the plan to clear Ollie was doomed to complete failure. Ollie himself had obviously not understood what he should do, and yesterday's baiting of the fifth year boys had, if anything, made it likely that there would be yet another fire for which Ollie would get the blame. What's more, Matt reflected gloomily, he had not had a chance to ask Ollie why he had taken so long to get from the children's home to Matt's house. The awful question mark was still there.

Kevin and the others were in high spirits. "Did you see the old boys planting their cabbages this morning?" asked Paul. "What a load of twits!"

"Makes me laugh," agreed Kevin. "All the mums and dads turning up like good little boys and girls to grow things for the teachers. Catch my old man doing that!"

"Who's going to have roast chicken, then?" grinned Paul.

"Just wait until Ollie lights his next fire—they can cook 'em on that!" said Micky. Several other boys laughed.

Rachel turned round to join in the conversation. "If you ask me," she said seriously, "the parents are silly, putting all that stuff together in the games pavilion. I mean, Ollie hates them coming in and out of the school—he thinks they're doing him out of a job. If there's anything he'll set on fire, it's the stuff for the Grand Auction."

Matt held his breath. The boys glanced at each other casually.

"I suppose he might," said Micky.

"Specially as he's probably going to lose his job, anyway," Rachel went on earnestly. "I bet he'll have one last go."

"Could be right," said Paul.

Kevin looked out of the window in a disinterested sort of way. Matt stared at him suspiciously. Was he trying to suppress a smile? It was difficult to be sure.

"When do you suppose he'll do it?" asked Paul airily.

"He probably won't," said Kevin at once. "So shut up."

As a parting shot, Rachel said, "Well, I think it's too awful even to think about."

"Oh, get lost," said Kevin, flapping a hand at her. "Kids like you can't think. Go and get mummy to change your nappy."

"And mind where she puts the pin!" shouted Micky as Rachel sat down, flushed but triumphant.

Danny drew a hand across his forehead and flicked away imaginary sweat. "Whew!" he said. "I didn't think you'd get away with that."

"Being a girl has advantages," said Rachel smugly. "They wouldn't have believed one of you but they think girls are silly, so they can't imagine I made it up."

Matt laughed. "You look like a cat that's had the cream," he said.

"A very practical cat, me," said Rachel.

Danny was looking rather worried. "Well," he said, "They've taken the bait. At least, I think they have. What happens now?"

"I don't know," said Matt soberly. "I really don't know. What if it's *not* them?" But nobody answered.

CHAPTER 12

Action!

Usually Matt looked forward to the weekend, but this one seemed like an unwelcome interruption. There was nothing he could do about Ollie, and he couldn't even be sure of seeing his friends because nobody had planned to do anything special. It all felt very uncomfortable, as if somebody had switched off the radio just as a tune was a couple of notes away from its end. He decided to make up Ollie's model aeroplane. At least it was something to do, and it gave him a good, solid reason for going to talk to Ollie on Monday morning.

He got the plan out of the box and spread it on the table. The pieces, as usual, were not quite accurately cut and he got busy with his balsa wood knife, trimming them meticulously.

"Matt," called his mother, "I'm going into Flaxton for some shopping. Do you want to come?"

Matt hesitated, then said, "Yes, please." It would pass away some time—and anyway, he needed some more balsa cement.

Everyone seemed to have had the same idea. He met Danny looking bored outside the supermarket and while they stood there talking, Rachel and Sue came along, with Sue's short-legged Jack Russell terrier on a lead.

"Hello!" said Rachel. "What are you doing?"

"Nothing," said Matt. "Bought a tube of balsa cement."

Danny nodded at the Jack Russell and said, "That's the sort of dog I feel like in Drama."

"That's the sort of dog you look like," Sue retorted, then ducked as he pretended to hit her.

"Did you come in with your mother?" asked Rachel. "Mine's in the library."

"Mine's in there," said Danny, indicated the supermarket's big windows behind him. "And so's Matt's."

"Well," said Rachel, "let's get them all together to go and have some coffee or something, then we can go in the park and Higgins can have a proper run off the lead."

"Stupid name for a dog," said Danny.

"My dad called him that." said Sue. "I wanted to call him Spot but Higgins sort of stuck."

Rachel's mother came along with an armful of books. "Hello again," she said as she saw them. "And what are you lot going to do?"

"Go in the park," said Rachel promptly. "You know Matt's mother, don't you? Will you take her for coffee and talk about houses or something? And there's Danny's mother, too—what does she talk about, Danny?"

"Shopping," said Danny gloomily. And his mother emerged at that moment from the supermarket with a laden basket.

"Do you know," she said to Danny, "salad cream has gone up six whole pence?"

Sue giggled and Rachel gave her a reproving glance. "Mrs Williams," she said politely, "this is my mother. Oh, you don't know me, of course, do you? I'm Rachel Greenberg, in Danny's form at school. Mum's name is Alice."

"Pleased to meet you," said Danny's mother, looking rather startled.

"How about some coffee?" said Mrs Greenberg as if she had only just thought of it. "We'll wait for Ann and she can come along, too. See you kids in the car park, O.K?"

"In about half an hour," said Rachel. As they moved away they heard Mrs Williams saying, "Goodness! They make up their own minds these days, don't they?"

"It's awful, being Saturday," said Matt as they walked across the grass with the little dog running circles round them.

"Frustrating," agreed Rachel. "I wonder what's happening at school, if anything. I wish it was in the middle of town like St Benedict's—I'd pop in and look."

"There'll be heaps of parents there today, doing scheme things," said Sue. "So nothing awful can happen."

"What about after dark?" said Matt.

Rachel shrugged. "Nothing we can do about it. We may as well forget the whole thing until Monday."

"It's so boring," said Danny. "What about going to the pictures? There's a James Bond on."

"That's a good idea!" said Rachel. "Let's go and see what time it starts. We can go round by the cinema on the way back to the car park."

Following in her wake, Matt glanced over his shoulder to where the distant roofs of the school were just visible as an erratic set of triangles across the fields on the far side of the park. Despite what Sue had said, he wished he could be there—just in case.

Matt felt quite excited about going to the pictures. It was a long time since he had been out with friends rather than with his mother, and they had decided to go to the early evening performance because the Greenbergs were going somewhere else in the afternoon. He did a lot more to his model aeroplane then had tea with his mother and was waiting by the window when Mrs Greenberg's car drew up with Rachel and Sue and Danny already in it.

"Bye-bye, love," said his mother, kissing him. "You will come straight home, won't you?"

"Yes, of course," said Matt rather impatiently. "Mrs Greenberg will drop me back. Don't *worry*, Mum! I'm only going to the pictures!" And he went out and got in the car.

Mrs Greenberg stopped outside the cinema where the bright lights cast a pool of radiance across the crowded pavement. "Looks as if there's a queue," she said. "I hope you'll get in all right."

"Of course we will," said Rachel, opening the car door.

"I'd quite like to see it myself," said Mrs Greenberg, "but we've got these friends coming over this evening. Look, Rachel, if you don't get in, ring me straight away and I'll come and pick you up."

"O.K.," said Rachel. "But the queue only goes to the corner, look." The others joined her on the pavement and Matt felt in his pocket to make sure the money his mother had given him was still there.

"See you later!" called Mrs Greenberg. "I'll be here when the film ends."

They waved, and she drove away.

The queue did not stop at the corner of the building. It went on down the alleyway at the side of the cinema—and on, and on.

"Oh, *blast*," said Danny disconsolately as they fell in behind the last people in the long line. "We'll *never* get in."

"It's a big cinema," said Rachel. "We might."

But as they neared the corner of the building in the patient, shuffling queue, a woman in a nylon overall came and flashed a torch along the people still waiting in the dark alley. "Full up now!" she shouted. "Sorry!"

Grumbling, the queue dispersed.

"Well," said Matt. "What do we do now?"

"Ring up Mum," said Rachel, shrugging. Then she added, "Unless—"

"Unless what?" asked Danny.

"Well—we might just have a look at the school, now we've got nothing else to do."

Matt's heart jumped with excitement. "Come on," he said, starting off at once.

Danny followed him but Sue said, "Are you sure we should? I mean—"

"It's all right, Sue," Rachel assured her. "We're not going to do anything dangerous. We'll just look, and if we see anything at all odd, we'll ring up my mum."

"Oh," said Sue, still sounding a little doubtful. "All right, then."

The park gates were locked at dusk, so Matt and the others set off along the dark roads which led out of the town, the houses thinning gradually as they approached the open fields. It seemed a very long way.

"The trouble with our school is it's not near anywhere else," said Danny, whose short legs were beginning to feel the strain.

"That's because it's new," said Sue. "The towns are all filled up with buildings already, so anything new has to be built in between the towns, miles from anywhere."

They walked on, and at last came to the winding drive which turned off the road and led to the school.

"No noise now," cautioned Rachel.

"Wish we had a torch," whispered Danny.

They walked carefully along the grass verge by the drive so that their footsteps should not be heard, and arrived in the bus parking place. The school buildings were silhouetted blackly against the streaky sky, where a band of red along the horizon showed where the sun had died. A blue light danced behind the drawn curtains at the caretaker's house, indicating that Mr Amos—and Ollie, Matt hoped—was inside, watching television. The school windows, on the other hand, were all black. The building seemed totally deserted.

"May as well just walk round it," murmured Rachel. "Now we're here."

Still moving very cautiously, they made their way through the orchard which flanked the sports hall with its old apple trees. Matt saw the pale blob of Rachel's face as she turned to indicate that they should cut across the games field, circling behind the school. He followed, but half way across the field she suddenly veered to the left, hissing, "Must check the pavilion."

The games pavilion, which at present housed the goods intended for the Grand Auction, was, like the orchard, a relic of old times. Built of white-painted wood, it huddled against the bank, its balcony looking out across the sports field. Shallow wooden steps led from the grass up to the balcony, and there was something about its gracious, rather spindly lines which evoked a sense of a more leisured age.

Matt followed Rachel across the grass and stood looking up at the silent building. Then he heard a rustle which seemed to come from beneath it, and cocked his head attentively. He felt, rather than saw, Rachel glance at him questioningly. Without speaking, he tiptoed across the grass and made his way towards the left hand side of the building. The others followed him. The pavilion was above the level of anyone standing on the field, and Matt knew that the sound had come from the big space below the wooden planking of the balcony. It was probably just a rat, he told himself; but all the same, the hair on the back of his neck prickled, and his heart was beating very fast.

Danny and the two girls joined him and they stood in a close group, straining to see something—anything—in the darkness. It was so quiet that the air seemed to hum. They could smell the hempen scent of the cricket nets which Mr Ellis had stored in the space below the pavilion while the building itself was otherwise occupied.

Suddenly Danny grabbed at Matt's arm and Sue gave a gasp. Matt had heard it too. Slow, quiet footsteps were approaching. Rachel had dropped to her hands and knees behind the shelter of the cricket nets, quickly followed by Danny. Matt grabbed Sue's hand and pulled her down to join the others in the scratchy, resin-smelling nets. As he did so he remembered Mr Gremmit talking about the firebugs pouring creosote before they set light to his yard. These nets smelled almost like creosote. They, too, would burn, as the builder had said, 'like fun'. Matt hardly dared to breathe.

A match scratched and flared. Its light seemed dazzling in the surrounding blackness and for a moment Matt had a glimpse of a crouched figure. Fury overcame him. "Come on!" he shouted, and leaped over the pile of netting in front of him. The figure, whoever it was, gave a grunt of fear, then fought. Matt was elbowed off but Danny had flung himself at the intruder's knees and was clinging on grimly. Something metallic fell from the figure's grasp and a strong smell of paraffin arose from all about them. Matt, galvanised into new action by the fear of the nets catching fire, hurled himself forward again. At the same moment Rachel, who had been groping about frantically, found a net's edge. "Sue!" she shouted. "Take this—pull it over him!" Matt found himself enmeshed with the unknown, struggling person as the girls heaved the net across the top of them both. Danny was somewhere underfoot and Matt was dragged off balance by the weight of the net. He and the intruder fell headlong, the girls on top of them in their determination not to let the firebug go.

Suddenly a powerful torch cut through the darkness. "Stay where you are, all of you!" shouted a voice.

"Mr Hazzard!" gasped Matt.

The headmaster strode across. Rachel and Sue scrambled to their feet and Matt sat up, trying to disentangle himself from the net. Danny wriggled free. The torch beam ran across the net-covered dark jacket of the stranger, who flung up an arm to cover his face. Mr Hazzard threw the net back and grabbed him by the collar. "Get up!" he ordered. "Who are you?"

Reluctantly, the man put his arm down and the torch picked out the shaggy hair and frightened blue eyes of—Ollie Withett.

"Oh, no!" Rachel almost sobbed.

Matt turned away. He felt rather sick.

"It's not me!" Ollie shouted. "I only came out to look round, then they jumped on me."

"You came to look round," the Headmaster repeated sadly, "with a box of matches? And paraffin? Don't say any more, Ollie. Danny, run across to Mr Amos and tell him to ring the police. Quick as you can."

Danny did as he was told.

"I've got a hurricane lamp," Ollie protested frantically. "That's all. It's here somewhere." He attempted to bend down and look among the netting but Mr Hazzard seized him by the arm and jerked him upright. It flashed unbidden through Matt's mind that someone had said only a few days ago that Mr Hazzard might not be as soft as he looked. It seemed like something remembered from when he was very small. Nothing would ever be the same again now. Matt was very close to tears and his legs felt shaky. He sat down among the cricket netting—and a hard, metallic object rolled gently down into the hollow he had made, and came to rest against his legs. It was a hurricane lamp. Matt picked it up.

"Mr Hazzard," he said with a glimmer of hope, "there *is* a hurricane lamp. It's here."

"The man from the fire service told Mr Amos to keep the current switched off at the mains when it wasn't needed," Ollie explained desperately. "And I thought I heard someone out here so I didn't light the lamp or they'd have seen me coming. Then when I got here it was all quiet and I thought it must have been a rat so I thought I'd have a look. And when I struck a match they all jumped on me. *Please*, Mr Hazzard, that's the truth. Honest."

Running footsteps diverted everyone's attention.

"Sir!" gasped Danny, tumbling in amongst them, "put the light out, quick! There's someone coming. Push bikes. They're putting them against the hedge. They didn't see me, far as I know."

Inky blackness engulfed them as Mr Hazzard switched off the torch. They waited tensely. Matt could hear Danny's rapid breathing and knew he was struggling not to make a noise. He put out a hand and gave him a friendly shove on the shoulder.

Then there were people coming. Although they were walking carefully, they were not as quiet as Ollie had been.

"Ssh!" breathed Mr Hazzard to the group round him. "Nobody move till I tell you."

They heard the subdued hollow clang of a can as the lid was removed, then a trickling sound, and the unmistakable reek of creosote drifted to their noses. Matt felt his limbs twitch with the desire to jump out and stop the marauders before they ignited the fearfully inflammable mixture of netting and creosote. Rachel wriggled stealthily backwards and Matt knew that she, too, was horribly aware of the danger.

A cigarette lighter flicked once, twice, then flared up, and the radiance of the small flame illuminated the intent faces circled round it. They were Kevin Evans, Micky Brent and Paul Arcot.

Mr Hazzard leaped up and shouted, "Stand still, you boys!" His torch beam picked them out as mercilessly as enemy aircraft in a searchlight and the boys flung up their hands to shield their dazzled eyes. Then they turned and ran.

"Don't chase them," said Mr Hazzard. "You may get hurt."

But Ollie had bounded out from his hiding place in the netting and was after the boys with greyhound speed. Matt heard thuds and shouts and Mr Hazzard yelled, "Ollie! Leave them alone! Come back here!"

"You're asking a bit much, sir," said Matt, clasping th hurricane lamp by its wire handle. The sense of elation made him want to laugh and sing. It was over! Ollie was all right!

A police siren grew rapidly louder as a police car with its blue light flashing swept in along the drive, followed by a police van. The bulkhead lights along the drive's edge leaped into brightness as Mr Amos switched them on, seeing the police arrive, and the scene was suddenly thrown into sharp relief.

The three boys were backed up against the hedge with Ollie standing menacingly before them. Micky was crouched on the ground, holding his knee in both hands, and Paul was bent double, clutching his midriff. Kevin's nose was bleeding copiously and, to Matt's sudden embarrassment, he was grovelling apologetically. "Oh, please, Ollie," he was whining, "give us a chance. I always liked you, really. We never meant any harm. And it wasn't us what done the one at the home, anyway. You *must* have started that one."

Ollie turned away in disgust as the police rushed up. "Kids," he said. "They're nothing but kids."

Matt and his friends watched silently as Mr Hazzard went over to the three boys and spoke to them briefly. After a few moments the police bundled them into the van and shut the rear doors. The blue light went on flashing and Mr Hazzard stayed by the van, answering questions while voices crackled through the two-way radios. Matt gave a little shiver.

"Well," said Rachel rather shakily, " we did it."

"Oh, Matt," said Sue, "I'm so glad it wasn't Ollie."

Matt couldn't say anything. His sense of elation had evaporated and, absurdly, he felt more than ever as if he was going to cry.

"Good thing it was me that went over to Mr Amos," said Danny cheerfully. "They'd have seen anyone bigger!"

Matt giggled instead.

Mr Hazzard came back with Ollie beside him and said, "Come over to the office, you people. We'll put the fire on and warm up a bit. I don't know why you were here but I certainly want to thank you."

"So do I!" said Ollie.

They started across the grass to the school, dreamlike in the dark, and Mr Hazzard called, "Mr Amos, could your wife make a hot drink of some kind for these people, please? If they feel like I do, they're in need of it."

"Yes, sir," said the caretaker. "For how many?"

"Six of us," said Mr Hazzard.

They reached the paved area and paused while Mr Hazzard fished for his keys and stopped to open the main door.

"Wasn't it exciting!" said Danny. "Better than going to the pictures!"

Nobody answered and, glancing at Sue and Rachel in the sudden glare as Mr Hazzard switched on the lights in the foyer, Matt saw that they felt as he did—relieved that it was over but somehow a little shaken by the whole affair.

In Mr Hazzard's brightly lit office with the electric fire glowing warmly, things seemed much better. They sipped hot, sweet cocoa and a policeman came in and wrote down all their names. Then he went back to the police car and they saw its tail lights follow the van away down the drive. After that they explained to Mr Hazzard about trying to go to the pictures and about their sudden alternative decision to come and look at the school instead.

"Well," said Mr Hazzard, shaking his head, "I must say, I'm glad you did. Although I really ought to scold you for taking such a risk."

A question had been nagging at the back of Matt's mind, and now he decided to ask it. "Sir," he said, "why were *you* here?"

"Me?" The headmaster smiled a little sheepishly. "Rachel's rumours had been running round like wildfire, if you'll pardon the expression. And the police had already told me that certain young gentlemen in the fifth year didn't give very convincing answers when questioned about the builder's yard."

"And then I told you about emptying the bin, and the paper towels on my bonfire," put in Ollie.

"*Did* you?" said Matt eagerly.

"Yes, he came and told me this morning when I came in to

see the parents working in the grounds," said Mr Hazzard. "And I had a look through the timetable to see if the boys concerned might have been out of their lesson and—er—decided that they might."

"What lesson was it, sir?" asked Danny.

"That is no business of yours, my lad," said Mr Hazzard firmly. "But I decided to keep a close eye on the school after that. I parked my car in the vehicle maintenance bay behind the workshops. I was there when you walked round the school on your way across to the pavilion—I could just see you against the last of the sunset. I nearly rang the police but I thought you looked too small to be the villains. So I walked through the school and came out this side to see what you were up to. And then, of course, I saw Ollie."

He turned to Ollie and said, "What I don't understand is, why you came out alone to look round. I told you this morning to make sure you had Mr Amos with you."

"He went to sleep in front of the telly," said Ollie simply. "He looked that peaceful, it seemed a bit much to wake him up."

"I woke him up all right!" grinned Danny. "He had the fright of his life!"

"Oh, gosh!" said Rachel suddenly. "What's the time?"

"Ten to nine," said Mr Hazzard. "Why?"

"Oh, is that all?" said Rachel. "I thought it was later. I must ring mum and tell her we're here or she'll go to pick us up from the cinema. But there's plenty of time—she won't leave for quite a while yet."

"Use my phone," said Mr Hazzard, indicating the telephone on his desk. "Ring her right away."

How quickly time had gone, Matt thought as Rachel dialled her number. All this had happened in less than two hours. It seemed impossible. Then he remembered a previous occasion when he had stood in this very office, worrying about another question of time. He glanced over at Ollie who was sitting on a chair with an empty cocoa mug clasped between his big hands.

"Ollie—" he said.

Ollie grinned. "What?" he asked.

"You know when you came to my house that night—well, why did you walk all the way from the children's home instead of getting the bus?"

Rachel had got through to her mother and was explaining volubly and with great drama why they weren't at the cinema, so Matt had to lean forward to hear the answer to his question.

"Why didn't I get on the bus?" Ollie repeated. He shrugged his shoulders. "Simple, mate. I hadn't got any money. Friday was pay day, wasn't it? But I went out of here too fast to think about that. All I had in my pocket was enough to get out there with Mrs Morecambe's coffee table. And I couldn't ask her for the fare back, could I? You can't borrow money off someone on their birthday."

"Of course not," said Matt happily.

"Mum's on her way here," reported Rachel, putting the receiver down. "And she says congratulations to everyone."

Lulled by warmth and cocoa and contentment, Matt stifled a small yawn. "*My* mum is going to be *frantic*," he said.

CHAPTER 13

A Red Face for Mr Watts

The school bus seemed strangely quiet on Monday morning. Matt looked at the empty back seats where Kevin and Micky and Paul usually sat, and knew when he saw them that the events of Saturday night were not a dream. It really had all happened. He should know by now that it was true, he told himself, after the police had come to his house yesterday to write down his part of the story. And after what his mother had said. "I was worried all evening about you. I should have known you'd get yourself into trouble. Only going to the pictures, indeed!" And so on. But she had got over it now, and Matt even began to feel that she was secretly rather proud of him.

"Where are the laughing lads today?" asked the driver as he pulled up in the bus park at school. "Playing truant, I suppose!"

"Something like that," agreed Matt.

Danny beamed and said, "They've been nicked for fire-raising!"

"No!" The driver was scandalised. "Now, that's a very serious offence. Dear, dear, dear." And they left him shaking his head.

Ollie was feeding the chickens, standing like a large, shaggy animal inside the wire netting of the run which the parents had built. Matt dashed across to see him. There were three brown eggs in a bucket by Ollie's feet. Ollie indicated them and said, "There you are. We can feed the whole school on those. A crumb each."

"I've brought your aeroplane," said Matt, holding up his carrier bag with the finished model in it.

"You didn't take long over that," said Ollie through the netting. "Let's have a look."

Carefully, Matt got the Spitfire out of the bag and held it up.

"Hang on!" said Ollie. He picked up the bucket and let himself out of the run, closing the door carefully behind him. Then he took the model in both hands and looked at it carefully. "That's really great," he said. "Beautiful job. You sure you don't mind the kid having it?"

Matt shook his head. "Of course not," he said. "That was the whole idea." There was a pause. "Mum says, would you like to come and have tea with us," said Matt. "After school today. And stay for the evening."

"Oh." Ollie frowned. "Dunno. Said I'd go and cut Mrs Abbott's lawn. She came out and asked me just now."

The bell rang, sounding from all over the school, and Matt said, "I'll have to go. Can you look after the model? I can't take it into Mr Potter's classroom—there's nowhere safe to keep it."

Ollie nodded. "Sure," he said, taking the bag with the aeroplane in it. "See you."

"Don't burn Mrs Abbott's house down!" said Matt.

Ollie grinned briefly. "Old bag," he said. And he set off across the grass, walking very carefully with his two fragile burdens; the bucket with the three eggs in it, and the model Spitfire.

Matt watched him with affection for a moment or two, then ran back to the school.

For once, Mr Potter's class was quiet as soon as the teacher came in. He stopped and looked at them with some surprise, and everyone giggled. He put his books down on his desk. "Well," he said. "What can I say?"

"Not a lot," said Danny.

"Oh, I think he ought to say something," Rachel argued.

"Make a speech," agreed Sue.

"Speech!" demanded everyone. "Speech!"

Mr Potter held up his hand. He cleared his throat theatrically and began, "Ladies and gentlemen! It is obvious that you have all heard about the heroic deeds of some members of our class." There were cheers and he waited for quiet before continuing, "Which have resulted in the apprehension of those responsible for the recent outbreaks of fire."

"What's he on about?" asked John Beasley.

"They got the firebugs," Stephen explained.

"Oh," said John. "Why didn't he say so, then?"

"I would like to congratulate all concerned," went on Mr Potter, "and it is a great relief to know that the school is safe from any further attacks." Then, amid renewed cheers, he abandoned his official pose and sat down on the edge of his desk with his hands in his pockets. "Quite honestly," he said as the cheers subsided, "I feel a bit shaken to think that people were being so malicious. And the worst of it is, we were all as bad. Even me, at one point. It's so easy, isn't it, to assume that rumours are true." He looked at Matt and said, "You stuck up for your friend, Matt, and I admire you for it."

Matt turned crimson, and Rachel said quickly, "Isn't Mr Potter lovely!" It had become a catch phrase, and everyone shouted with laughter.

"Oh, Lord," said Mr Potter, with a return to his usual confusion, "it's first year assembly this morning and I haven't done the register yet. Shut up, everyone." And, but for some irrepressible giggling, they were all quiet.

Mr Hazzard was very complimentary about the way in which the fire raisers had been caught, but, to Matt's relief, he did not mention their names or ask them to come out in front of the assembly. Although he felt immensely warm and happy to think Ollie was no longer suspected, Matt was still rather embarrassed to think that he had got himself involved in something so dramatic. Rachel, however, was in her element. She told everyone about it in great detail, even risking a whispered account during Mr Watt's Maths lesson—with disastrous results.

"Rachel Greenberg!" thundered Mr Watts, "Have you completely taken leave of your senses?"

"No, sir!" said Rachel innocently.

"Then why are you behaving like an utter hooligan in my lesson? You are not invited here to entertain us with the unsavoury details of your personal exploits, even if they *have* attracted some favourable comment from those in authority. It is clear to me that you regard yourself as a genius but I, for one, do not share that opinion. *Stand up when I am talking to you!*"

Rachel got to her feet obediently. Although her cheeks burned, she kept her chin up and her lower lip stuck out obstinately. She would not show hurt feelings easily.

"Yes," said Mr Watts, surveying her. "You are the kind of person who thinks herself above the rules which are good enough for the common herd. You and your kind are nothing more than conceited, lawless trouble-makers, thoroughly anti-social and a nuisance to everyone you come in contact with. When you have left school you are welcome to join the band of useless drop-outs which plagues our society but meanwhile you will behave yourself and do as you are told, do you understand?"

Unnoticed by Mr Watts, the door had opened during this tirade and now Mr Hazzard came in, followed by a photographer and Angela Purling, the reporter who had come to Rachel's sale.

"Well, Rachel," said Mr Hazzard easily. "You're standing up in welcome already, I see. You know Miss Purling, don't you?"

"Yes, sir," said Rachel, with one eye on Mr Watts, who seemed about to have a heart attack through an excess of fury.

"I was so glad to get your message on my answering machine," said Angela Purling to Rachel. "Awfully sensible of you to ring the office yesterday and put it all on tape. When I heard it this morning I came down here straight away."

The photographer spotted Matt and said, "Oh, you're the chap who made the model aeroplane. My little grandson loved it. Just the job!"

"Oh, good," said Matt.

Mr Watts turned away and stared out of the window, gripping his thumbs behind his back.

"It's all right if we take some pictures, is it, Mr—er?" Angela asked him. But Mr Watts did not turn round.

"Mr Watts," said Mr Hazzard icily. "This lady is speaking to you."

"What? Oh, I beg your pardon," said Mr Watts, turning

to face the headmaster. "I must admit, I did not realise that the proceedings concerned me in any way."

Mr Hazzard gave him a very straight look and said, "I think the *school* concerns you, Mr Watts?"

The senior master gulped. "Oh," he said, "yes, of course." And he managed a smile.

"Now," said Angela Purling brightly, "can we have the four heroes all sitting together? Everyone move round a bit—that's right. And the rest of the class in the picture, too. We want it to look quite natural. Let's have teacher bending over Rachel's book, shall we?"

Reluctantly, Mr Watts took up the position assigned to him.

"Oh, you mustn't look disapproving!" cried Angela merrily, patting Mr Watts on the shoulder. "Let's have a nice smile—she's your prize pupil, remember!" Mr Watts produced a glassy grin.

"Smashing," said the photographer. "Stay like that. Now another one. No, don't stop smiling. The kids are all falling about so we want the teacher looking happy, too!"

Angela Purling wrote down all the names and listened to Rachel's story complete with interruptions from all the others, then folded up her notebook. "That's marvellous," she said. "It should be in this evening's Star."

"No mention of the culprits' names," Mr Hazzard cautioned her.

"Of course not," she assured him. "They'll come before the juvenile court, so we can't use their names." She turned to Mr Watts and smiled at him. "Thank you so much," she said.

Mr Watts nodded. He did not smile back.

When the visitors had been ushered out, a babble of conversation arose.

"That's enough!" snapped Mr Watts. But, for once, nobody took any notice. The bell rang for the end of the lesson and they all stood up, stuffing Maths books into their bags and talking and laughing as though they were already at liberty outside. Not waiting for them to leave, Mr Watts got up and walked out of the room.

Matt grinned. "Talk about saved by the bell!" he said.

Rachel glared after Mr Watts. "He's *not* lovely," she said. "But never mind. Just wait till he sees his picture in the paper!"

Miss Harker was on duty at break and Rachel's face lit up when she saw her. "Come on!" she said to Matt, and rushed across.

"Hello, Miss Harker!" she said kindly.

Miss Harker smiled. "Hello, Rachel. I hear you've been very clever," she said. "You and your friends."

"About the firebugs? Oh, yes," Rachel said casually. "Miss Harker, can you settle an argument for us? You know on Tuesday afternoons you have us for R.E. last two periods—who do you have before us? Matt says it's third year and I think it's fifth."

"Fifth year," confirmed Miss Harker. "Set three." Her smile faded as she looked at Rachel and knew why the question had been asked. Matt remembered what Mr Hazzard had said on Saturday night about Kevin and his friends being out of a lesson, and wondered what he had said to Miss Harker.

"You're always right about everything, Rachel," he grumbled quickly. "It gets really boring." He turned away and called back, "See you, Miss Harker."

"Thanks," said Rachel to Matt when they were out of earshot. "Poor thing. I wish I hadn't asked her."

"Why?" asked Danny, who had just run up to join them.

"She let Kevin and those out of her lesson," explained Matt. "I expect they said they wanted to go to the toilet. And that's when they started the fire in the bog."

"Just as well," said Danny cheerfully. "It all helped to find out who was doing it."

"I still feel sorry for her," said Rachel. "We'll make everyone be really nice to her tomorrow."

"You'll be lucky," said Matt. "Hey—wasn't it great, that reporter arriving just then! Mr Watts'll be furious, having his photo in the paper!"

"Serve him right," said Rachel.

Ollie stumped past with his wheelbarrow. Matt and

Danny waved and Rachel called, "Hello, Ollie!" Without stopping, Ollie turned his head slightly sideways and blew a large bubble of pink gum which exploded with a crack.

"Isn't he awful!" said Rachel admiringly. "Fancy your mother asking him to tea, Matt—she won't like him a bit."

"He's not coming," Matt told her.

"Oh." Rachel looked at him, not sure if she should be sympathetic. "Do you mind?"

"Not really," said Matt. He glanced at Ollie's retreating back and smiled.

"What's so funny?" asked Danny.

The double peal of the school bell saved Matt from having to answer. What could he have said, anyway? Ollie was just Ollie.

"Race you!" said Rachel, setting off across the grass at top speed.

There was no hope of catching her, so Matt didn't even try. He sauntered across the field in the sunshine, suddenly aware that he was feeling amazingly happy. School, he thought, was all right—sometimes.